THE CHURCH IN THE TEMPESTS
The First Millennium of the History of the Church

ROBERTO DE MATTEI

CALX MARIAE
PUBLISHING

Original title: *La Chiesa fra le tempeste. Il primo millennio di storia della Chiesa nelle conversazioni a Radio Maria*

© 2012 Sugarco Edizioni, Milano, Italy

Roberto de Mattei's talks on the history of the Church, which are collected in this book, were originally given on the *Radio Maria* programme "Radici Cristiane" between January 2011 and April 2012. An updated introduction is included in this English edition.

Translated into English by Peter Mitchell

Scripture quotations are from the Douay-Rheims Bible.

English edition © 2022 Voice of the Family, Calx Mariae Publishing

Calx Mariae Publishing is an imprint of Voice of the Family, London, United Kingdom.

All rights reserved.

ISBN: 978-1-8384785-3-7

www.voiceofthefamily.com

CONTENTS

Introduction		9
I	The first three centuries of the Church	19
II	The crisis of the fourth century	39
III	The monks conquer the world	60
IV	Pagan Rome and Christian Rome	79
V	Why the Roman Empire fell	98
VI	The conversion of the European nations	113
VII	The prime of Christian Europe	134
VIII	The reform of the Church of the year 1000	154
IX	The spirit of the Crusades	174

INTRODUCTION

In the Gospels, Jesus uses many metaphors to describe the Church He founded. One of the most apt is the image of a boat threatened by a storm (Mt 8:23-27; Mk 4:35-40; Lk 8:22-25). This image is often taken up by the Fathers of the Church and the saints who speak of the Church as a barque battered by the waves, which dwells, so to speak, amidst the storms but without ever letting itself be submerged by the waves.[1]

Saint Catherine of Siena, for example, made a promise to go to Saint Peter's Basilica every morning to pray before Giotto's mosaic on the pediment of the ancient basilica which depicted the scene of the barque of Peter in the storm. On one particular day, 29 January 1380, towards the time for Vespers, Jesus detached himself from the mosaic and approached Saint Catherine, who was absorbed in ecstasy, and placed the stricken boat of the Church upon her weak shoulders. She fell to the ground senseless, oppressed by so much weight. This was Catherine's last visit to Saint Peter's, having always exhorted the pope with the words: "Take the helm of the barque of Holy Church."[2]

Benedict XVI, in his turn, used the metaphor applied by Saint Basil to the circumstances of the Church after the Council of Nicea,[3] and compared our times to a night-time naval battle in a stormy sea, and in his homily for the feast of Saints Peter and Paul on 29 June 2006 he described the barque of the Church as "ripped apart by the winds of ideologies" but unsinkable and secure in her course.

The battle rages in the night, as Saint John Bosco saw in his famous dream of the "Two Columns in the Sea".[4] Peter's ship is assailed, and the pope is seriously struck once, and then a second

---

[1] See, for example, St Augustine, *Discourse* 75, 3.4 and 4.5.
[2] See, for example, St Catherine of Siena, *Letter* 373.
[3] St Basil, *De Spiritu Sancto*, 30, 77.
[4] Eugenio Pilla, *I sogni di Don Bosco*, Cantagalli, Siena 1979, pp. 193-196.

time; he falls down and dies, but a new pope, overcoming every obstacle, anchors the boat to two columns that rise out of the sea: one on which shines the Eucharistic Host, the other surmounted by the Immaculate Virgin. The enemy ships flee and smash each other as the Church celebrates her triumph.

Today the barque of Peter appears to be at the mercy of the storm. Those aboard, facing the tempestuous waves, look with trepidation at her captain, the Vicar of Christ. Like its founder, the Church consists of a human element — visible and external, and a divine element — spiritual and invisible. It is a society that is at once visible and spiritual; temporal and eternal; human on account of the members that make it up and divine on account of its supernatural origin, end and resources. The pope is the one in whom the Church's visibility is concentrated and condensed. This is the meaning of the expression of Saint Ambrose: *Ubi Petrus ibi ecclesia*,[5] which presupposes the other expression attributed to Saint Ignatius of Antioch: *Ubi Christus, ibi ecclesia*.[6] There is no true Church outside the one founded by Jesus Christ, who continues to guide and assist it invisibly while its Vicar governs it visibly on earth.

The primacy of the pope's government, together with the infallibility of his magisterium, constitute the foundation on which Jesus Christ has instituted His Church and on which she will remain steadfast until the end of time. This primacy was conferred on Peter, the Prince of the Apostles, after the Resurrection (Jn 21:15-17) and was recognised in him by the early Church, not as a personal and transitory privilege but as a permanent and essential element of the divine constitution of the Church, to which Jesus gave a monarchical form to ensure her indefectibility.

The barque of Peter does not have a collegial head, just as there is no permissive moral license within her. Yet conciliarism, condemned by Pope Eugene IV at the Council of Florence (1439)

[5.] St Ambrosius, *Expositio in Psalmos*, 40.
[6.] St Ignatius of Antioch, *Smirnesi*, 8, 2.

and by Blessed Pius IX at the First Vatican Council (1870), has never been eradicated from the Church. In the post-conciliar era "collegiality" was the watchword of an egalitarian and democratic vision of a governmental structure, based on the role of one or more synods, which was set against papal "centralisation". Petrine primacy was contrasted with "synodality", elevated to the rank of normative principle. Synodality, collegiality, decentralisation are the words that today express the attempt to transform the monarchical and hierarchical constitution of the Church into a democratic and parliamentary structure.

In order to democratise the Church, the innovators try to strip it of its institutional aspect and reduce it to a purely sacramental dimension.

On the sacramental level the pope, as bishop, is the same as all the other bishops. What sets him above all the bishops and grants him supreme, full and immediate power over the whole Church is his power of jurisdiction, or government, which distinguishes him from any other bishop. The office held by the pope does not represent a fourth degree of holy orders after the diaconate, priesthood and episcopate. The Petrine ministry is not a sacrament, but an office, because the pope is the visible Vicar of Jesus Christ.

The "reform of the Church" so often spoken of today is first of all a "decapitation" of pontifical authority, replaced with a sort of "parliament" of the Church, with currents and parties fighting each other, as already happens because of the centrifugal forces at play. In reality, the universality of the Church requires the exercise of a strong central authority, and if today there is fragmentation and anarchy this is certainly not due to an excess of power but, if anything, to the weakening of papal governance in favour of bishops' conferences and peripheral and local realities. The crisis that we have before us is also a consequence of this process of erosion of pontifical centrality. On the other hand, the great reformers of the Church, like Saint Gregory the Great in the sixth century and

Saint Gregory VII in the eleventh century, have always accompanied their work of renewal with a clear affirmation of papal primacy. Whoever presumes to "reform" the papacy undermines the juridical foundation of the Church and, with it, her moral law; while whoever loves the Church can only unite the defence of the natural and moral law to a defence of papal primacy against conciliarist and localist tendencies.

The forefront of this revolution within the Church is the so-called "synodal path", under the leadership of the Church in Germany. The assembly of German bishops, meeting in Frankfurt from 3 to 5 February 2022, approved by majority a document in which the pope is asked to revise the discipline of celibacy and the ordination of married men, including the authorisation of current priests to take wives as a matter of course. At the same time, another vote approved the non-exclusion of women from the ordained ministries, meaning their access to the diaconate and priesthood. The assembly then pronounced itself, by a large majority, to be in favour of a "sexual modernisation" of the Church that would include the possibility of blessings for all couples, including homosexuals and the divorced and remarried.

The Frankfurt assembly also decided that there should be more joint decision-making in the election of Catholic bishops in Germany, in such a way that bishops may truly represent their base. "Synodality" is the name of this democratisation of the Church that accompanies its moral collapse.

The co-responsibility of Pope Francis in this process of secularisation is driving part of the conservative and traditionalist world to reject the authority of the supreme pontiff. The error seems to be that of confusing the man with the institution, and of distancing oneself not from a pope inadequate in terms of his office of government, but from the office itself, dissolving the primatial nature of the Petrine ministry. In order to reject synodality, one would end up rejecting the very visibility of the Church, which has become a charismatic and acephalous entity.

The Church cannot be saved in this way, in part because only Jesus, and no one else, can save the Church. Men, beginning with the Vicar of Christ on earth down to the last member of the faithful, can only collaborate with divine grace, which comes to us by the influence of the Holy Ghost and drives us to a radical fidelity to Christ and His law.

We cannot save the Church; we can only love her and serve her, imitating the example of all those who in the course of history have given their life for her. Those who claim to save the Church really want to construct a Church according to their own opinion, different from that of Christ. The Church instituted by Christ is a visible body, made up of different members united by means of visible bonds; and it is monarchical, because it is founded on the primacy of Peter. Neither the pope nor the bishops can change the law of the Gospel handed down from Jesus Himself. This law, communicated by Jesus to the apostles, excludes women from holy orders, subjects the laity to the clergy, and calls all men and women to continence and sacrifice.

The present crisis does not arise from this model of doctrine and life which tradition hands down to us but rather from a departure from it. All of the heresiarchs over the course of the centuries, have advocated a pseudo-reform of the Church that would disfigure her face. But the only true reform is to rediscover tradition, which is none other than the perennial teaching of Christ, and living it coherently as the saints have done.[7] In the difficult periods for the Church, it was the saints, not the heretics, who saved her.

The heretics today always contrast the early Church with the supposed regression of the medieval and tridentine Church, but the history of the Church of the first millennium offers us quite

---

[7] Cf. Roberto de Mattei, *Apologia for Tradition - A defense of Tradition grounded in the historical context of the Faith*, Angelus Press, Kansas City 2019.

a different picture. History, which is the teacher of life and the Christian faith, teaches us through the example of the martyrs that the truth is not negotiable and must be witnessed to, if necessary, with blood. The monks and hermits remind us of the renunciation of the world and the necessity of constant union with the Lord, in silence and prayer. The activity of the apologists shows us how their apostolate is exercised not only in positively expounding the faith but also in refuting prejudices and errors with the weapons of polemic and controversy. The foundations of Christianity were laid in the first millennium of Christian history and the Christian sovereigns and princes who created the European nations offer us an example of how one can Christianise the world without belonging to it.

The example of the Crusaders is the most generous of all, because they offered their life for the Church, ignoring the trials they would have to undergo in order to carry out their vocation to the full. The spirit with which they went forth for the liberation of the Holy Sepulchre is the same spirit that we ought to ask for today in order to liberate the Church and civilisation from the evils which afflict her. Let no one be scandalised. The beauty of the Church lies in the variety of the vocations that are expressed within her. The number of vocations is as large as the number of rational creatures, but they all converge toward a single goal, which is the glory of God, the First Cause and Final End of the created universe. In the famous passage in her *Story of a Soul*, Saint Thérèse describes the variety of vocations that she would like to embrace. It is worth re-reading, in order to fathom the great love for Jesus and the Church with which she was imbued.

> "To be Your spouse, Jesus; to be a Carmelite; to be, thanks to union with You, the mother of souls, should be enough for me. But it is not so! ... It is true, these three privileges are my vocation: Carmelite, spouse and mother; but I feel

other vocations in me: I feel within me the vocation of the warrior, the priest, the apostle, the doctor, the martyr; in short, I feel the need, the desire to accomplish all of the most heroic works for You, Jesus.

"... I feel in my soul the courage of a Crusader, of a papal Zouave: I would like to die on a battlefield for the defence of the Church ... I feel within me the vocation of the priest: with what love, O Jesus, would I carry You in my hands when, at my voice, You descended from heaven! With what love would I give You to souls! But, alas, while desiring to be a priest, I admire and envy the humility of Saint Francis of Assisi, and I feel within me the vocation of imitating him in refusing the sublime dignity of the priesthood.

"O Jesus, my love, my life! ... How can these contrasts be reconciled? How can the desires of my poor little soul be realised?

"... Ah, despite my littleness, I would like to illuminate souls like the prophets and doctors have done! I have the vocation to be an apostle ... I would like to travel the earth, preach Your name, plant Your glorious Cross on infidel soil! But, O my Beloved, one single mission would not be enough for me: at the same time, I would like to announce the Gospel in the five parts of the world even to the farthest islands ... I would like to be a missionary not only for a few years, but I would like to have been one since the creation of the world and to be one until the end of the ages ... But above all I would like, O my Beloved Saviour, I would like to shed my blood for You to the last drop!

"... Martyrdom: behold the dream of my youth! This dream has grown within me behind the cloister of Carmel. But also here, I feel that my dream is madness, because I would not be able to limit myself to desiring only one form of martyrdom ... It would take all of them to satisfy me!

"... Like You, my Adorable Spouse, I would like to be scourged and crucified.

"... I would like to die flayed like Saint Bartholomew ... Like Saint John, I would like to be immersed in boiling oil; I would like to undergo all the tortures inflicted on the martyrs. With Saint Agnes and Saint Cecilia I would like to present my neck to the sword, and like Joan of Arc, my beloved sister, I would like to whisper Your name at the stake, O Jesus! ... Considering the torments that will befall Christians at the time of the Antichrist, I feel my heart leap, and I would like those torments to be reserved for me ... Jesus, Jesus! If I wanted to write all of my desires, I would have to take Your Book of Life: there all the actions of Your saints are recorded, and I would like to have done all of those acts for You.

"... O my Jesus, what will You answer to all of my follies? Is there a soul that is smaller or more powerless than mine? ... And yet precisely because of my weakness, You were pleased, Lord, to hear my little childish wishes, and today You want to hear other desires greater than the universe."[8]

The words of Saint Thérèse form a manifesto of the Catholic faith to be contrasted with the heterodox proclamations of the neo-modernists. This is the true freedom of the children of God, never separated from the truth. Each man and all peoples have

---

[8]. St Thérèse of the Child Jesus, *Opere Complete*, Libreria Editrice Vaticana, Vatican City, 1997, p. 221.

their own vocation, but so does every epoch, which is simply the precise way in which it is called to fulfil the will of God in the present moment. In the midst of today's storms, God asks us to do what is lacking in our time and in the Church herself: to pray and to fight. The soul of every apostolate is the interior life, which is the soul's impulse towards God, all the more important when He is absent from a world that contemplates only itself.

But praying is not enough. The motto of Catholic Action used to be: "Prayer, action, sacrifice". Action and sacrifice today may be summed up as the battle against the external and internal enemies of the Church. It is for this battle against evil that the Church is called "militant".

"He that hath my commandments, and keepeth them; he it is that loveth me" (Jn 14:21). But today the law of God is transgressed and mocked, and those who love God fight so that His commandments may be freely observed and publicly professed. We do not fight to impose the faith, because nothing is more free than the act of faith, but we fight to protect this faith from evil and error, because nothing is more true than the Christian faith. The Lord wants us to pray and fight for Him, in a conflict that is now global and has assumed a total and definitive character.

Orare et pugnare — to pray and to fight. May this motto gather together Christian warriors from every corner of the earth and unite them in the defence of divine law against the enemies of God and His Church who, as the "Fiery Prayer" of Saint Louis Marie Grignion de Montfort reminds us, have already launched their battle cry: *Sonuerunt, frenduerunt, fremuerunt, multiplicati sunt* — "They have shouted; they have gnashed their teeth; they have raged; they have swelled their ranks". But with the great saint of the Vendée, we repeat: *Dirumpamus vincula eorum et projiciamus a nobis jugum ipsorum. Qui habitat in caelis irridebit eos* — "Let us break their bonds asunder: and let us cast away their yoke from us. He that dwelleth in heaven shall laugh at them" (Psalm 2:3-4).

NOTE TO THE READER

In this book are gathered various talks on the history of the Church given by the author to *Radio Maria* for the programme "Radici Cristiane" between January 2011 and April 2012. Every chapter faithfully reproduces the spoken conversation. Since this is not a scientific text, there are no footnotes, and at times there are no references to the works that are quoted. The author, wishing to echo Catholic tradition without any pretence of originality, has drawn from many historical, theological and spiritual works, including *The Liturgical Year* by Dom Prosper Guéranger, conversations on the "Saint of the Day" with Plinio Corrêa de Oliveira until his death in 1995, the three-volume work of Abbé Joseph Lemann *La Dame des Nations dans l'Europe catholique*, and the first two volumes of the *History of the Church* by Henri Daniel-Rops, of which some passages are reproduced verbatim, without any references. The author makes his own the words of Dom Prosper Guéranger (1805–1875), the great abbot of Solesmes, who defined the Catholic historian as the one who "judges facts, men, institutions from the point of view of the Church; he is not free to judge otherwise, and this is his strength".[9]

[9.] Dom Prosper Guéranger, *The Christian Sense of History*, Calx Mariae Publishing, 2022, p.52.

CHAPTER I

The first three centuries of the Church

1. Christianity faces the Roman Empire

We live in an era of which every aspect is in crisis: economic, political, but above all spiritual and moral. It is this aspect of the crisis that interests us the most: that which touches our life, because we consist not only of physical bodies, as most of our contemporaries believe (and live accordingly), but of body and soul, and the soul is not only the most noble part of our being, it is also what gives life to our being, that through which we live and breathe. We have a soul, and so we have or we ought to have a spiritual life. This spiritual life comes from the gift of faith which is infused in us through baptism and is nourished by grace, which is communicated by the sacraments of the Church. Everything which concerns the Church touches our faith, and everything which touches our faith has consequences for our soul and for the souls of those who are dear to us. This is why we ought to be interested in the Church and her history, because understanding what happened yesterday will help us to live today.

When we speak of the Church, we ought to remember that there are actually three Churches, which together form one single Church: the Church Militant composed of all the baptised who profess the same faith under the same pastors; the Church Suffering, or penitent, which is made up of all the dead who are being purified in purgatory, waiting to enter heaven; and finally the Church

Triumphant, made up of the saints who already live in eternal happiness in divine glory. Together these three realities form the Communion of Saints, which is a dogma that we profess in our Creed.

In order to understand the history of the Church, not only yesterday, or two thousand years ago, but also — and above all — today, we ought to keep the word "militant" ever present in our mind. The Church Militant means the Church that fights. Saint Paul explains in many passages of his letters how the life of the Christian is a *bonum certamen*, a "good fight", which is to be fought "as a good soldier of Christ Jesus" (2 Tim 2:3). "Let us therefore cast off the works of darkness," he says, "and put on the armour of light" (Rom 13:12). It is true that the Church on earth suffers, but before all else she fights. She suffers when — and because — she fights; but for the Church, and for us who are Christians, the time of suffering is in purgatory more than on earth. We are not born in order to suffer but rather to fight and to win, even if suffering accompanies us our entire life. However, this suffering should not please us, because it is a consequence of sin. Life on earth is a battle, a battle between two cities: the City of God and that of the devil. The Church and her enemies, as Saint Augustine says in the *City of God*, fight against one another until the end of time.

We wish therefore, to recall the most important episodes of this battle, which is renewed each day and in which we should not be spectators but actors. We must imagine the setting of the world to be like a great theatre in which the angels and saints are watching from heaven, with Jesus and Mary sitting in the royal box. Let us choose therefore, to do our part, studying the script of history.

Let us begin by speaking about the first centuries of the Church, so far away and yet at the same time so near. Those early centuries were a time of persecution and martyrdom, but precisely for this reason they were a time of struggle: the struggle conducted first by the apostles and then by their successors in order to fulfil the command of Christ, to spread the Gospel to the farthest corners of the earth.

At that moment, Christianity had before it the Roman Empire, the greatest empire that history had ever known. Christianity and the Roman Empire were, so to speak, the same age because, although the history of Rome began 753 years before Christ with the foundation of the city by Romulus and Remus, the birth of the empire occurred thanks to Emperor Augustus Caesar, during whose reign Jesus was born in the Roman province of Palestine.

The Roman Empire and nascent Christianity found themselves facing one another. There was neither agreement nor compromise between them, only a battle without respite between these two realities. The battle was not declared by Christianity but by the empire, which did not tolerate the claim to absolute truth made by Christianity, with its message of radical and integral salvation.

The first great confrontation was the trial of Jesus, which was initiated by the Jews in the Sanhedrin, but was then brought before Pilate, the supreme judge of Palestine. Pilate, who represented the Roman Empire, condemned Christ to crucifixion. This is not the place to discuss whether the greater responsibility belonged to him or to those who incited him to crucify Christ. What is more important is to emphasise here that Jesus wanted to show from the very beginning that there would be a radical incompatibility between the Church and the world. The Passion and Death of Jesus was the model of all suffering and physical pain, but above all of spiritual and moral suffering that Christians would have to endure throughout history.

The Roman Empire not only condemned Jesus at the hands of Pilate, but after Pilate was removed from Palestine it continued to condemn Christ, refusing to recognise Christianity with the status of *religio licita*, a "licit religion", in the empire.

The persecution against Christians began in Palestine in AD 34 with the stoning of Stephen, as desired by Caiaphas, and continued with the death of James, the son of Zebedee, the first of the apostles to be martyred, sentenced to death by King Herod Agrippa I. The apologists speak of Emperor Tiberius (14–37) demanding a report of these events from the procurator of Galilee, Pontius Pilate. According to Tertullian, Pilate's report drove Tiberius to ask the Roman Senate to recognise the divinity of Jesus and to grant Christianity the status of *religio licita*, but the Senate refused to grant this recognition. From the very beginning, the Roman senatorial aristocracy manifested its aversion to Christianity and fed the persecutions against it, especially in the upper echelons of society, while popular antipathy against Christianity was stoked by the Jews, as the Acts of the Apostles recalls (19:23 ff).

2. The beginning of the persecutions

The large-scale persecutions against the Christians began in the year AD 64. On the night of 18–19 July, the trumpets of the city sentries blasted forth in Rome, sounding the fire alarm. A violent blaze had broken out in the popular district of the Circus Maximus, amidst the grocery stores and fabric shops. Fed by reserves of olive oil and combustible materials, the fire suddenly reached the entire area surrounding the Palatine and Caelian Hills. The people tried to put it out in vain. For six days and six nights the flames engulfed Rome. Four of the fourteen districts of the city were burned to the ground, and six others had only portions of wall remaining and clusters of uninhabitable houses. Only four districts could be said to have remained intact. The French historian Henri Daniel-Rops gives a helpful reconstruction of this event.

The emperor at the time was Nero (54–68), having succeeded his adoptive father Claudius (41–54). Today an effort is being made to rehabilitate his memory, but Nero was the man who had his mother Agrippina killed; the same Agrippina who had given him the throne by a criminal act. Nero was the man who had repudiated his legitimate wife, Octavia, by despicably slandering her before having her executed. He was the man who, due to his cruelty, was now accused by the *vox populi* of even being responsible for the fire. It was said that his servants had been seen running through the lower quarters of the city with torches in hand. Suetonius relates the rumour that during the fire Nero went up to the top of the tower of Mycenae and, dressed in a theatre costume and with a lyre in his hand, sang a poem he had written about the taking of Troy and the fire laid by the warriors of Agamemnon.

What is certain is that Nero vented his fury on the Christians, accusing them of being responsible for the destruction of Rome. Overnight, at his order, the prisons were filled with Christians, to the point that Tacitus writes of the "vast multitude" who were arrested: words that offer us a precious indication of the extent of the presence of the new faith in Rome, less than 35 years after the death of Christ.

A terrible fate, however, awaited the Christians of Rome. The victims would not only be tortured, decapitated and crucified in the Circus of Nero, which was located in the same place as the present Basilica of Saint Peter. Hunting parties were held in the imperial parks, in which the Christians were the prey, sewn into the skins of ferocious beasts and torn to pieces by dogs. The most barbaric and indecent mythological scenes were recreated, in which the Christians, playing the parts of "extras", were exposed to every sort of outrage. And in the evening, Nero dressed in the livery of a coachman and drove his chariot along avenues overrun by brutal mobs, illuminated with human torches: Christians covered with pitch and resin and set on fire while still alive.

Saint Clement of Rome, the future pope (†97), who had perhaps been an eyewitness to this, retained an enduring memory of the horror of this night of 15 August of the year 64, and Tacitus himself confessed that such an excess of atrocities against the Christians attracted the compassion of those of upright conscience.

Saint Peter and Saint Paul both died in the course of this terrible persecution, along with thousands of other Christians. Today the Mother Church of Christianity stands over the tomb of Peter after whom she is named. And in the very place where Nero sought to silence the voice of Peter for good, the words of his successors continue to be addressed to the peoples of the world.

The death of Nero was followed by a quiet period until the reign of Emperor Domitian (81–96). We are now looking at the year 90 after the birth of Christ, and in the 27 years since the death of Nero, the Christian faith had greatly strengthened its position, spreading to the highest levels of society.

This time the first to be affected were members of the aristocracy. Flavius Clement was for a long time under suspicion for his lack of collaboration with the emperor in matters of official cult and, according to Suetonius, he was condemned to death "on a very slight suspicion". His wife Domitilla was relegated to the island of Pandataria and to this day her name still graces the wall of one of Rome's most evocative catacombs. Domitilla and her husband belonged to the Flavian *gens*, the most noble family of Rome, and they were cousins of Emperor Domitian. This did not save them. Nor was the consul Manius Acilius Glabrio spared. He was a member of Roman aristocracy most distinguished for his righteousness and valour; his family cemetery on the Via Salaria would become the most ancient Christian necropolis.

Glabrio was a Roman senator and consul in the year 91. Domitian suspected that he was a Christian and put him to death. Eusebius writes that the emperor harboured a grudge against Glabrio, as shown by the fact that he had called him to the *Juvenalia* on Mount Albano and forced him to fight with a huge lion. Glabrio not only did not suffer any injuries, but he killed the lion with a masterful stroke. These were the Christians: slaves as well as aristocrats, defenceless women as well as men capable of killing lions with their bare hands.

It was also Domitian who exiled John the Evangelist to the island of Patmos and, in Palestine, sought out the descendants of the family of the one who was called "King of the Jews", having the sons of Jude the Apostle transported to Rome for interrogation, which however came to nothing.

Christians were surrounded by hatred which was stoked by circles of Jews and pagans alike. It was a hatred without any precise motivation, but when the *vox populi* is raised, as Daniel-Rops observes, it is not always the *vox Dei*, nor necessarily the voice of reason and common sense. Christian rites, which were very poorly known, were intentionally interpreted in the worst possible way. Accusations against the Christians, earlier on instigated by the Judeans who had persecuted and crucified Jesus, were extremely wide-ranging. They are expounded by Minucius Felix in his work *Octavius*, by Tertullian in his *Apologeticum* and by Athenagoras in his book *The Embassy*, or *A Plea for the Christians*. The accusation of atheism originated in the Christians' refusal to sacrifice to the gods of Rome; that of incest because of the familiarity that existed between those who called each other brothers and sisters; and the kiss of peace which was given in the Christian assemblies led people to imagine improper relationships. The Christians were accused of worshipping a donkey's head, of adoring the genitals of their priests, of slaughtering a child and drinking its blood in the rite of Christian initiation; of not having altars, temples and images; of gathering in secret; and of being the cause of the calamities of the empire. The Eucharistic sacrifice, with formulas like "this is my body; this is my blood" made people think of some unimaginable cannibal ritual.

In vain did apologists dismantle these absurd accusations; calumny continued to circulate and to spread. Tertullian tells us how in his own city, Carthage, a short time before the composition of the *Apologeticum*, a picture was presented to the public that depicted the god of the Christians with the ears of a donkey and the feet of a goat, holding a book in his hand and wearing a toga. "If the Tiber overflows," the apologist wrote, "if the Nile does not flood the countryside, if the sky withholds rain, if the earth quakes; if famine, war or plague strikes, immediately there is an outcry: 'Christians to the lions! Death to the Christians!'" And he adds: "The majority of men have a special hatred against the name of Christian which is so blind that it is impossible to give favourable testimony about a Christian without mixing it with the reproach of bearing this name. One says: 'What an honest man that Gaius Seius is; what a shame he is a Christian!' And another adds: 'For myself, I find it strange that Lucius Titius, a man who is so enlightened, has immediately become a Christian.' No one asks if it might be possible that the reason Gaius is honest and Lucius is enlightened is because they are Christians, or if perhaps the very reason that they became Christians is due to the fact that one is honest and the other enlightened."

The Jews were among the first accusers of the Christians. They too worshipped a single God, but although the image of their God was not depicted in the Pantheon, they were accepted because they represented a nation for which Rome had passed laws of toleration. The Christians were not a nation, merely Roman subjects. The majority of them were deprived of Roman citizenship, at least up until the Edict of Caracalla in 212, through which all subjects of the Roman Empire became Roman citizens.

3. *Christianos esse non licet*

All of these accusations, however, were of an extra-judicial nature, and did not influence the juridical mentality of the Romans. It was necessary to give a foundation to the calumnies, and this was contained in a simple formula, the *Institutum Neronianum* of which Tertullian speaks, summarised in the judicial aphorism *Christianos esse non licet* — it is not permitted to be Christian.

Many studies have attempted to demonstrate that the Christians were persecuted for civil reasons under the law which punished crimes of treason, or for reasons of social tranquility (punishing resistance with *coercitio*, considered a remedy for public order). In reality, the underlying reason was religious, and this remained the juridical foundation of the persecutions. "The motive which explains the beginning as well as the continuation of the persecutions is hatred against Christians," writes Ludwig von Hertling, recalling the affirmation of Tertullian: "As soon as the Truth entered the world, it aroused hatred and aversion by its simple existence."

It should be recalled that the Roman religion was essentially political, as the Law of the Twelve Tables states: "No one may have gods on his own account, either new or foreign, if they are not recognised by the State." The *Imperium Romanum* was above all a political power, but the veneration of the gods was one of the duties of the state and constituted an important element of Roman law. The duty of the state was that of regulating the public cult of the gods, independently of the private religion of its citizens. Christianity was accused of atheism, because it denied the religion of the "goddess Rome" incarnated in the emperor god. Everyone was free to worship other gods as long as they adored Rome and Caesar: otherwise a crime of sacrilege was committed.

Already in 42 BC, Augustus (27 BC–AD 14) had his adoptive father Julius Caesar deified by a decree of the Senate. A divine veneration for themselves was later demanded by Emperors Caligula (37–41) and Domitian (81–96). From the third century the cult of the emperor was imposed as a manifestation of the political and religious loyalty of his subjects. Christianity never opposed the established power which it held, and still holds, to be received from God; but it opposed this power when it became a dominion that usurped the rights of God. The Christians' loyalty to Rome is founded in the thirteenth chapter of Saint Paul's *Letter to the Romans* and in the second chapter of the *First Letter of Saint Peter*; it is also expressed in the Gospel in the words of Jesus Himself: "Render therefore to Caesar the things that are Caesar's, and to God the things that are God's" (Mk 12:17).

In AD 112, the legal status of Christianity in the empire was defined for the first time by correspondence between the imperial legate Pliny the Younger and his superior, Emperor Trajan (98–117). The question which Pliny posed to the emperor may be summarised as follows: "Is it the very name of Christian that must be punished?" In this case would it be necessary to condemn to death not only those who professed the doctrine but even those who renounced it? Pliny suggested that a policy of clemency, urging people towards apostasy, could have better effects as regards the social and religious peace of the province. In the *rescriptum* with which Trajan responded, he defines the line of conduct that the official should follow: "It is not necessary to search for Christians, but if they are denounced and confess themselves to be such, they are to be punished. If someone, however, denies being Christian and proves it by praying to our gods, let him be pardoned." Trajan's *rescriptum* thus imposed a measure of clemency to anyone who apostatised.

Beyond the greater clemency shown by Trajan by comparison with his predecessors, it remains clear that the juridical foundation of the persecutions was in the sole fact of calling oneself a Christian: not in *being* one but in *proclaiming* oneself to be such, because it was enough to deny being a Christian and to offer sacrifice to the emperor in order to obtain pardon. As Tertullian observed well in an ironic phrase: "The Christian must be punished, not because he is guilty, but because he is discovered, even if he was not to be sought out."

But since the *nomen* was condemned, and not the crimes that could be attributed to that *nomen*, it was enough to reject the *nomen* of Christian in order to obtain pardon, which was not the case with those who committed other crimes embraced by the Roman penal code.

The policy of Trajan guided that of his successors in the following century and a half. It was not licit to be, or rather to say that one was, a Christian. Every Christian was a candidate for martyrdom. It depended on the individual emperors, however, whether to apply the law with greater or lesser severity. This explains how the first three centuries were not an era of systematic persecutions. There were periods of bloody persecutions, but also periods of great tranquility in which the Roman authorities left Christians free to conduct their own lives.

For their part, the Christians accepted the Roman institutions (Rom 13:1-7; Tit 3; 1 Pet 2:13-15), prayed for those established in power (1 Tim 2:1-2), paid taxes, and respected the laws of the State. The Church of the first centuries therefore was not a hidden and clandestine Church. The Christians were known, their authorities (bishops, priests, deacons) were known, their ideas in broad terms were partly manifest. The Christian philosopher Saint Justin Martyr (c.100–165), for example, opened a public school in Rome; he published his writings and was able to direct his *Apologies* to Antoninus Pius, Marcus Aurelius, and Lucius Verus, before being arrested for his faith.

Christians lived in their own families, exercised their professions like every citizen, and gathered for religious functions in their modest places of worship within the city walls. They followed the rite of inhumation, or burial, of the body, and not that of the cremation of their dead, and they had subterranean cemeteries, later called catacombs (from the Greek *katátumbas*). The catacombs were not secret places where the Christians hid but sepulchral areas where they were buried. Roman law recognised indiscriminately everyone's *ius sepulcri*, even for condemned criminals, whose remains the judge could consign to those who requested them for burial.

The age of the persecutions which began with Nero grew to a climax over the following three centuries, albeit at irregular intervals. After Domitian and Trajan, the African Septimius Severus

(193–211), at the beginning of the third century, issued a decree for the first time which prohibited conversion to Christianity. The famous school of Alexandria was closed, and many Christians were martyred (including Perpetua and Felicity, who were martyred in Carthage along with four other catechumens). The edict of Severus was enforced also under his son Caracalla (211–217), especially in Africa. Alexander Severus (217–235) was more tolerant. His mother Julia Mamea drew near to Christianity and was in contact with Origen and Hippolytus.

Maximinus of Thrace (235–238), the first of a long series of soldier emperors, sought to destroy the Church by an edict condemning bishops, priests, and deacons to death. In 249 a coup hatched by anti-Christian forces brought Decius (249–251) to the throne in place of Philip the Arab (244–249), who was a Christian. Origen emphasised the turning point during the reign of Decius, who resolved to erase all traces of Christianity. He instituted a special commission in each city and issued an edict in 250 ordering that all citizens of the empire were to burn incense before the pagan deities and participate in sacred banquets before the public authorities. Whoever refused was imprisoned and subjected to every sort of torture, up to and including death. What Decius wanted to obtain at any cost was the apostasy of Christians, the denial of their faith. Some escaped the threat by fleeing, and others apostatised. Thus originated the problem of the *lapsi*, that is, those Christians who, in order to escape death, offered incense to idols, but later repented. Among the many martyrs in Rome was Pope Fabian (240–253). "From this moment on," wrote Origen, "the persecutions no longer took place in a sporadic manner, as before, but in a widespread and generalised way." Decius's successor Gallus (251–253) did not persecute the Church but ordered all citizens to offer sacrifice to the god Apollo. Popes Cornelius and Lucius died in exile.

Emperor Valerian (c.253–c.261) sought to strike the leaders of the Church, convinced that by destroying the highest levels the foundation would also dissolve. For this reason, he issued a new edict (258) by which capital punishment was imposed on the leaders of churches and on Christians of noble birth, and all gatherings for worship of any sort and in any place were forbidden. Another pope, Saint Sixtus II (257–258) was seized while he was presiding over a liturgical ceremony in the catacombs of Saint Callistus and was beheaded along with the four deacons who were assisting him. Lawrence the Deacon was killed four days later on 10 August 258 and buried in the Campo Verano on the Via Tiburtina.

In the second half of the third century there was a truce for about forty years. The son of Valerian, Gallienus (261–268), revoked the edict against the Christians. There was a period of peace under him and his successor Aurelian (270–275), who adored the sun god. But at the end of the third century, the Dalmatian Emperor Diocletian (284–305) unleashed the final and most violent persecution. In 297 it was decided that the army must be purged of all Christians. Between 303 and 304 Diocletian issued four edicts with which he wanted to annihilate Christianity. The first edict in 303 ordered the destruction of church buildings, while the Christian nobles were deprived of their dignity and the plebeians were denied their liberty. In the summer of 303 the second and third edicts followed; clergy were arrested and forced to offer sacrifices. Not all of these provisions were implemented, but in 304 a fourth edict ordered that the entire population of the empire must offer sacrifice to the pagan divinities on pain of death. The majority of the martyrs who were later honoured in liturgical worship came from this persecution (Sebastian, Pancras, Agnes, Soter, Protase and Gervase, Marcellinus and Peter, and many others).

4. The testimony of the martyrs

The ancient Christian accounts of the persecutions are usually divided into three groups: *Acta* (that is, the official account of the trial), *Martyria* and *Passiones*, which are documents of a private nature, and *Gesta*, historical accounts issued after the end of the persecutions. The first pagan literary account of the persecutions of Christians dates back to Tacitus (the *Annales*, around 115) and Suetonius (the *Vita Neronis*, around 122).

The martyrs offered their testimony to Christ in two ways: by word and by blood. We recall a considerable number of arrested Christians who took advantage of the occasion of their trial to publicly profess their faith. At times it was a very simple affirmation, like that heard from the lips of the African martyrs: "I am a Christian!" Or when asked to identify themselves: "What is your name?" — "Christian! This is enough!" At other times it was a more explicit act of faith, such as that of Saint Justin in Rome, in 163: "We adore the God of the Christians. We believe that He is the One God, Creator from the beginning who orders every creature, both visible and invisible. We believe in the Lord Jesus Christ, the Son of God, proclaimed by the prophets, sent to save men, the Redeemer Messiah, the Teacher of sublime lessons."

Among the most renowned martyrs was Saint Ignatius of Antioch, owing to the significance he gave to his own martyrdom. Condemned in Antioch along with his two companions, Rufus and Zosimus, Ignatius was sent to Rome to be devoured by lions. Knowing the destiny that awaited him, he demonstrated an enthusiasm which can only have a supernatural explanation. He wrote to the Christians of Smyrna: "Under the blade of the executioner or among the ferocious beasts, I am as close to God as I will ever be." In the face of the most frightening fate imaginable, his only fear was that he would be spared. He cried out: "Since the altar is ready, let me make my sacrifice! Let me become prey for the wild beasts! It is through them that I shall attain God. I am the wheat of God: in order to become the pure bread of Christ, I must be ground by the teeth of the wild beasts."

A very popular book in the Middle Ages, the *Legenda Aurea* or *Golden Legend*, interpreting the additional name "Theophorus" which Ignatius had during his life, affirms that when his heart was opened, the name of Christ was found written on it in letters of gold.

Under the reign of Emperor Antoninus half a century later, Polycarp, another great saint and bishop of the East, would meet the same end. Polycarp had known Ignatius, and after his death gathered together his letters and meditated on his example. We possess many accounts of his trial and death, through a letter that the community of Smyrna sent to their brethren in Phrygia, following their request to tell them about these events as soon as they had taken place. Polycarp was an octogenarian, but there is no age limit for giving testimony to the Spirit, and often God gives to the weakest the strength to fight.

The proconsul urged him:

- Swear! Reproach Christ, and I will set you free.
- 86 years I have served him, and he has done me no wrong. How can I blaspheme my King and Saviour?
- Swear by the fortune of Caesar!
- You flatter yourself and hope to persuade me. In truth I tell you: I am a Christian.
- I have wild beasts at my disposal.
- Give your orders. We, when we change, do not change from better to worse; it is beautiful to pass from evil to justice.
- If you do not repent, I will make you perish by burning on a stake, since you disdain the wild beasts.
- You threaten me with a fire that burns for an hour and then is extinguished. But do you know the fire of justice that must come? Do you know the chastisement that will devour the wicked? Go, do not delay! Decide as you wish.

Another renowned martyrdom took place between 178 and 180: that of Saint Cecilia. Cecilia belonged to one of the most noble and ancient families of Rome, the *gens Caecilia* which throughout the centuries of the Roman Republic had won itself honour with glorious deeds. Before the executioner she proclaimed: *"Non possumus*! [We cannot.] Rather than living in pain and abandonment, we prefer to die in supreme freedom. And it is this truth which we proclaim that torments you; you who work so hard to make us lie…"

When Perpetua, a young woman of noble birth, was arrested in Carthage accused of being Christian, she still had her father and her mother, two brothers, one of whom was a catechumen, and she had an infant at the breast. Her elderly father was a convinced pagan who multiplied his efforts to bring his daughter back to the traditional religion. When he heard that his daughter was to appear before the tribunal, he ran in haste from his villa in Tuburbo.

> "The father said to her: 'My daughter, have pity on my white hair, have pity on your father, if I am still worthy to be called your father. If it is true that these hands have raised you to the prime of life; if among all my children you are my favourite, do not surrender me to the mockery of the world. Think of your brothers, your mother, your aunt, your son who will not be able to live without you. Return from your decision and do not ruin your entire family. None of us will have the right to speak as a free man, if you are condemned.'
>
> 'Behold,' said Perpetua, 'what my father has said in his affection. And at the same time that he was kissing my hands, he threw himself at my feet; he called me no longer "daughter", but "lady". And I suffered seeing my father in this state. He alone of all my family did not rejoice over my passion. I sought to console him, saying to him: "Know that on the stage of the tribunal what will happen is God's will. We are not our own masters, but we belong to God."'

Another day, the poor father presented himself at the tribunal with Perpetua's child in his arms: 'Have pity on the white hair of your father and the youth of your child. Sacrifice for the salvation of the emperors.' Perpetua refused and declared herself Christian. But since her father stayed by her side, Hilarion chased him away and had him struck with a blow of a rod. 'This blow that my father received,' the martyr said, 'wounds me as if I had been struck, so much have I suffered for this father who is already old and so unhappy.' Finally, the day of execution approached. One last time the old father came to see his daughter and Perpetua concluded: 'Pain consumed him, and in his pain, he tore his beard, threw himself on the ground, and prostrated himself with his face against the ground. And I wept over the misfortunes of his old age.'" (*Passion of Perpetua and Felicity*, V/VI).

5. Martyrdom and Christian combat

In the Christian vision, martyrdom is the most perfect act of charity, since it makes us perfect imitators of Jesus, according to the words of the Gospel: "Greater love than this no man hath, that a man lay down his life for his friends" (Jn 15:13).

The concept of martyrdom is inherent in the very life of the Christian. Jesus says in his great discourse on the mission of the apostles: "I send you as sheep in the midst of wolves" (Mt 10:16), and also: "Beware of men. For they will deliver you up in councils, and they will scourge you in their synagogues. And you shall be brought before governors, and before kings for my sake, for a testimony to them and to the Gentiles" (Mt 10:17-18).

The specific meaning of the term "martyrdom" is connected with "giving witness" which reaches its apex in the profession of the phrase *"Christianus sum"*. Witness is the essence of martyrdom, and this ought to be made publicly even to the shedding of blood.

The witness of the martyr presupposes and confirms the testimony of the One who "was born and came into the world to bear witness to the truth" (Jn 18:37).

That which makes the martyr such is not a violent death, but the fact that death is inflicted in *odio fidei* — in hatred for the Christian faith. This element of intention distinguishes the Christian holocaust from any other sacrifice. The martyr must be put to death because of his fidelity to one of the principles of faith or morals which the Church infallibly teaches. It is not death that makes the martyr, says Saint Augustine, but the fact that his suffering and his death are ordered to the truth. Death undergone in witness to the truth is the essence of martyrdom.

Today also there are truths and moral values for which one must be ready to give up even one's life. "This witness," John Paul II taught, "makes an extraordinarily valuable contribution to warding off ... a headlong plunge into the most dangerous crisis which can afflict man: the *confusion between good and evil*, which makes it impossible to build up and to preserve the moral order of individuals and communities. By their eloquent and attractive example of a life completely transfigured by the splendor of moral truth, the martyrs and, in general, all the Church's Saints, light up every period of history by reawakening its moral sense" (Encyclical *Veritatis Splendor*, n. 93).

Martyrdom, like all suffering, presupposes combat. We have already emphasised this. The fact that the Christian life is a battle is one of the concepts that most often resonates in the New Testament where we read: "For he also that striveth for the mastery, is not crowned, except he strive lawfully" (2 Tim 2:5). After all, the original meaning of the word "gospel" (from the Greek *euangélion*, good news) is the announcement of military victory, in this case the victory of Christ over evil and the powers of darkness.

The epic of the martyrs of the first three centuries shows us the intimate union that ought to exist between the Bridegroom and the Bride, between Christ and the Church, which is His Mystical Body. Saint Paul says that the husband must love his wife as Christ has loved the Church. The greatest expression of love is to offer one's life for the beloved. Jesus did this for the Church, and the first members of the Church, the apostles and their successors, wanted to do the same for Christ. It is in this love, this sacrifice, that the fruitfulness of the Church is found, and by means of the blood of the martyrs generated thousands of Christians and began her conquest of the world.

After three centuries of persecutions the Roman Empire began to decline and inevitably at the same time, the Church of Christ started to rise. In the person of His Vicar, the pope, Christ began to reign in that same city of Rome in which the greatest empire in history had been established. The epic of the martyrs is not an episode of history that has been concluded in time. This lesson is alive and present at the Colosseum, the Flavian Amphitheatre constructed by Vespasian. Today it is a tourist destination, but at one time it was a place for meditation where Saint Leonard of Port Maurice had a great cross erected, and where the young girl Saint Thérèse of Lisieux, visiting Rome on pilgrimage, knelt down to kiss the earth, as if she were looking for the fragrance of the blood shed by the martyrs in the soil of the Colosseum.

Martyrdom is above all a witness to the truth. It calls us to publicly profess our faith. It is an act of fidelity; fidelity even unto death to the Word of Christ transmitted by Him to the apostles and by them to their successors. Thus, it is fidelity to the Church and her tradition: a tradition that is the truth of the Gospel handed down, by word and in writing, from one generation to the next, right up to our own day. We are the heirs of the Christians of the first century, and we must imitate their spirit. It is not easy, but we must ask for this grace. If they were faithful, it was thanks to the Holy Ghost who transformed and sanctified them. We too can be transformed and sanctified, asking as they did for the intercession of Our Lady, Mother of the Church, Queen of the Apostles and Martyrs, who is the help of all those who in the course of history have fought the good fight.

Radio Maria, 21 September 2011

CHAPTER II

The crisis of the fourth century

1. The "Constantinian shift"

In order to live as good Christians, it is necessary to know the Catechism, which summarises the teachings of the Gospel, the precepts of the Church, and the law that must be respected in order to gain eternal life, because as Jesus says, "he that hath my commandments, and keepeth them; he it is that loveth me" (Jn 14:21), and in order to observe them one must first of all know them.

Today we have become illiterate in religious matters, and this is one of the reasons that the law of the Lord is not observed and that Jesus is not loved. But while it is necessary to know the Catechism, it is equally important to know the history of the Church, because the Church is a living organism, the Mystical Body that embraces all of human history and has at its heart the Incarnation of the Word, an event which took place over two thousand years ago in Palestine, when God, the one true God, became man in the womb of a Virgin. This event radically changed history, which from then on has reckoned its years with reference to the birth of Christ.

We live in the era that since then has been called Christian, and we have the grace of having been born as Christians: the two millennia that are now behind us are our history and our roots. We ought to know that history, because the history of the Church is the history of the Bride of Christ, who in her earthly pilgrimage retraces the life of her founder and spouse. We are part of this Mystical Body, which is the Church, and in order to live in our times we must know the way that the Christians who preceded us, who are our brothers in the Communion of Saints, have lived out the Gospel, faced trials, and fought the good fight. It is good to remember always that the life of the Church was never peaceful and serene: it has known trials, battles and persecutions, in conformity with the words of the Gospel: "Behold I send you as sheep in the midst of wolves" (Mt 10:16).

The first three centuries of the Church run from the Ascension of the Lord to the advent of Emperor Constantine in the year of Our Lord 312. It was the era of persecutions, or as some have called it, the era of the catacombs. It was an era in the Church's history, her infancy, in which Christians did not have free citizenship in the Roman Empire but were persecuted and repressed.

The emperors wanted to eradicate the Church and were convinced that they would succeed, because the Christians refused to adore the Roman emperor as a divinity and repeated that it was necessary to give to God what belongs to God and to Caesar what belongs to Caesar (Mt 20:21, Mk 12:17, Lk 20:25). Since then to our own days, this maxim has been one of the hinges of Christian thought.

For three centuries, from Nero to Diocletian, the persecutions raged, until the day when a young general Constantine (274–337), who was vying with Maxentius to conquer the throne of Rome, routed his rival's army at Saxa Rubra on the outskirts of Rome.

It was 28 October 312. On the eve of a battle that would not only change the fate of the empire but of the entire Church, Constantine had a vision and a dream. A shining cross appeared in the sky along with the words: *In hoc signo vinces* (In this sign thou shalt conquer). And then, as is related by both Eusebius and Lactantius, the Lord appeared to Constantine during the night, exhorting him to imprint this cross on the banners of his legions. Thus it was under the sign of the cross that Constantine faced Maxentius and at the Milvian Bridge at the gates of Rome, he annihilated the enemy army and ascended to the imperial throne. This date marked an epochal turning point, destined to be known to history as the "Constantinian shift".

In the following year, 313, Constantine granted full liberty to Christians by the Edict of Milan. They would no longer be persecuted: they would be able to walk with their heads held high in the streets of the empire, build their churches, celebrate their liturgical rites, and open schools, hospitals and shelters for the elderly, orphans and the weak. They would be able to serve in the army, in the judiciary and in the Senate. They would be able to Christianise society, transform it from pagan to Christian, and infuse the life-giving breath of the Gospel into the sick body of a dying empire. It was the hour of triumph, celebrated by the first Christian historians such as Eusebius of Caesarea.

And yet, during these years of the invincible ascent of Christianity, from the Edict of Constantine in 313 to that of another emperor, Theodosius (347–395), who declared Christianity the one religion of the Roman Empire in 380, a new dreadful storm lashed the Church: a tempest so terrible as to make some wish to return to the era of the persecutions. It was more terrible than that earlier trial because this time the enemy was not external but within the Church herself: it was not physical violence that assailed her but heresy, which is worse than violence, because it causes not the death of the body but the death of the soul.

2. The heresy of Arius

Ever since its birth, the life of the Church has been accompanied by errors and heresies. The father of heresy is considered to be Simon Magus, the gnostic who wanted to purchase the charisms of Peter and the apostles and who crashed to the ground as he sought to fly through the air with the help of the devil (Acts 8:9-10). But no heresy had such widespread diffusion and such serious consequences as the one that appeared at the beginning of the fourth century and which seemed to shake the Church to her very foundations. This heresy was Arianism, which takes its name from its founder, the priest Arius (256–336), a Libyan by birth who came as a youth to the patriarchal city of Alexandria. Ordained deacon around 308 and a priest two years later, in 313 Arius was placed in charge of the church of Baucalis, one of the quarters of Alexandria, from where he preached a new doctrine.

God, said Arius, is one — eternal and not generated. Apart from God, everything is a creature, including Christ, the Word of God. He declared that the Word, the Second Person of the Most Holy Trinity, is not equal to the Father but created by Him, as an intermediate being between God and man. Jesus Christ thus was not Son of God by nature but only by grace and adoption. The Holy Ghost in turn was the first creature of the Son and therefore inferior to Him.

Arianism was a heresy that struck at the heart of the Trinitarian mystery, undermining the very foundations of the faith and falsifying the deepest sense of the message of the Gospel. If Jesus Christ is not really God, then there is no longer any incarnation nor any redemption of humanity. By denying the mystery of the incarnation, the heresy of Arius made Christianity more easily accessible to the pagans, who were amazed at the idea of a God becoming man, but, thinking of the divinised heroes of the ancient tradition, they could easily comprehend that a man by his own merits could become God. On the other hand, within the Church herself some theologians had maintained that the Father and the Son were one and the same person: this was the heresy of Sabellius, which although it had been condemned remained an active influence.

Finally, as a further help to the success of the heretical enterprise, there was also Arius's extraordinary ability to play on the sense of certain words of scripture, such as the affirmation "God created me" which is found in the Book of Proverbs and which the Arians understood as a prophecy of the Messiah; or again the passage of the Gospel according to Saint John where Jesus says: "The Father is greater than I" (Jn 14:28).

For more than sixty years, a fierce battle unfolded in the Christian East and West, in which the loftiest questions regarding the divinity of Christ were disputed and men faced each other in a struggle to the death in defence of the truth. If today we do not understand this struggle, writes the historian Henri Daniel-Rops, is it not perhaps because our era, weaker in faith and colder in temperament, no longer experiences with the same intensity the need for the knowledge of God?

When, around 320, the Patriarch of Alexandria, Saint Alexander, heard of the opinions of the priest who was under his authority, he invited Arius and his opponents to appear before a synod, where their positions would be judged by one hundred bishops from Egypt and Libya.

At the synod, which took place in Alexandria, Arius presented himself with proud confidence. He knew that he was supported by many who thought as he did, or close enough. Among these was Eusebius, the bishop of Nicomedia, a man of boundless ambition. He was able to influence the emperor because of the geographical position of the city where he lived, which was the eastern capital of the empire. But if Arius was determined to do battle, there was another great example of a Christian warrior who stood in Arius's way: Athanasius, a young deacon who was only twenty years old, the secretary of bishop Alexander. As the French historian Daniel-Rops observes, Athanasius's fragile appearance hid an indomitable soul, and he would become the greatest adversary that the heretic would encounter in his error.

The synod took place in a heated atmosphere. Apart from two or three bishops, all of those present were in favour of Alexander, that is, of orthodoxy, and against the heretic Arius. There were dramatic moments: for example, when the heresiarch, constrained by his logic, affirmed that Christ, as a creature, could have potentially sinned, the assembly emitted a groan of horror. Arius was condemned together with other clergy who had aligned themselves with his positions. He received a formal order to submit or to resign. For several weeks he sought to preserve his position as a priest, but he realised that, in order to continue the battle, he needed to leave

Egypt, so he abandoned his parish to seek support outside his diocese. Up until this point, the matter had been a local disturbance, the likes of which the Church had experienced on many occasions, but it was now about to become a vast movement which would spread throughout the entire Christian East.

Under the pretext that Arius had been persecuted by his bishop, the ambitious Eusebius of Nicomedia summoned him. When Alexander heard of this, he sent a letter to his principal colleagues giving an account of the matter and formally accusing the prelate of Nicomedia of intrigue. What had been an Egyptian affair was now transformed into a battle between two opposing parties in the heart of the empire.

During the winter of 323–324, no Christian in the East could have been ignorant of the fact that a crisis was about to break out which promised to be very serious. The bishops wrote to each other about the affair, some siding with Arius, others against him. Alexander was reproached by Eusebius of Caesarea. The heresiarch himself, in order to shuffle the deck, disseminated a *symbolon* or creed summarising his theses, in which he skilfully wrapped them in so many expressions with double-meanings, misunderstandings and ambiguity, that many decent people could be led into error. This has always been the tactic of heresies: to shy away from sharp and clear expressions so as to mask their error with a veil of ambiguity and confusion.

3. The Council of Nicea

In the autumn of 324, the Emperor Constantine had definitively defeated his brother-in-law Licinius and the East was now under his dominion as much as was the West. But, entering into the city of Nicomedia, he found a threat of division in the very heart of the Church. He was frightened by it and pondered the matter during many sleepless nights. He finally decided to settle the problem once and for all. His ecclesiastical counsellors, above all Hosius of Corduba and the prelates of Antioch, persuaded him to gather a plenary assembly of all of Christianity in order to fully judge the affair, an assembly over which Constantine himself was to preside.

The Church had long been familiar with councils as an institution. The first Council was held in Jerusalem in 49, when Saint Paul and the apostles had together examined the approach to take in the face of the problem of the Judaizers. In the primitive Church, whenever serious points of discipline had to be established, they were addressed by regional meetings, and in fact in both Africa and Italy these meetings had taken place regularly in order to maintain ties between the leaders of Christianity. In the East these meetings were more intermittent, but many had taken place in Alexandria, Antioch, and even in Ancyra in the heart of Asia Minor. There was an idea in the air that a Council would reunite all of Christianity, that it would make the unity of the Church concretely present through a general meeting. Constantine adopted the idea with joy. He was seeking the religious peace of the empire. The universe, the *ecumene*, as they said in Greek, had only one head: the emperor. The Council which was to reunite the Church would be universal. It was thus decided to hold the first "Ecumenical Council".

During the winter of 324–325 preparations were made for the meeting. The place that was first proposed was Ancyra, but it was decided that access to the inland city would not be easy, and that the climate of the Anatolian highlands was too cold for a spring session. And so Nicea was chosen, a city in Bithynia, near to Nicomedia and also to Byzantium, which had begun to be transformed into the capital of the empire. The First Ecumenical Council of the Church was thus held in Nicea in the year 325, convoked by Emperor Constantine.

The historian Eusebius writes that "the flower of God's ministers came from all over Europe, from Libya and Asia" and that a single house of prayer, as if it had been enlarged by divine power, united Syrians, Cilicians, Phoenicians, Arabs, Palestinians, as well as people from Egypt, the Thebaid, Libya, and Mesopotamia. There was also the bishop of Persia, and there were Macedonians, Thracians, Achaians, Epirotes, and even "the most distant" had come, "and from Spain, for example, a most illustrious person". There was Hosius of Corduba, Cecilian of Carthage, who came from Africa, and from Italy came Mark, a Calabrian bishop. Pope Sylvester I (314–335), who had not been able to attend the Council due to his advanced age, was represented by two Roman clerics, Vitus and Vincent.

What was the total number of those delegated from all of Christianity? Eusebius of Caesarea says that there were 250, adding that they were accompanied by many priests, deacons, and acolytes who could not all be counted. Saint Athanasius gives another number: 318, which has become the traditional reckoning. It was, at any rate, a considerable assembly both because of the number and even more because of the quality of its members. Famous men were seen: the thaumaturges Spiridion and Jacob of Nisibis, who were said to have raised the dead; the confessors of the Egyptian faith, Potamon of Heraclea and Paphnutius of Thebes, who had both lost their eyes in the persecution of Maxentius, and also Paul of Neocaesarea, whose hands had been mutilated by the application of red hot irons by order of Licinius.

The opening session took place on 20 May 325 in an atmosphere of enthusiasm. More than ten years had passed since the end of the era of persecutions, and now the persecuted were the triumphant. Eusebius describes the imperial inauguration, the gala dinner given by Constantine for the Fathers, and the pomp with which he presented himself to them on that historic day that marked the definitive end of the era of persecutions. Ten years earlier for most, just one year earlier for others (those from Licinius's territory) life had still been impossible and the threat was constant. Now, there was the splendour of the palaces, the majesty of the ceremonies,

II THE CRISIS OF THE FOURTH CENTURY

and the guard of honour who presented arms before the Christian dignitaries. The emperor had paid the expenses of the Council Fathers, providing them with horses, carriages, and any material goods they needed. It was clear that it was an occasion marked by immense emotion and gratitude.

The discussions began, presided over by Constantine. As soon as the truly grave matters were addressed, however, it became clear that there were two opposing tendencies which were irreconcilable.

We will follow the reconstruction of Daniel-Rops. Arius was in the corridors and led the group of his partisans with clever tactical advice. He was supported in a more or less concrete way by about 15 bishops in the assembly, including Eusebius of Nicomedia, who was about to reconcile with Constantine. A series of subtle manoeuvres took place. Arius had his friends read a plea that he himself had prepared, in which he cunningly glided over the contestable points of his theses, enveloping them in a vocabulary that was intentionally ambiguous and imprecise. A group of bishops tried to mend everything, using only terms from scripture to define Christ: could one not say, for example, that the Word is "of God", that He is the "Son of God", that He is "the strength and image of the Father"? To which the Arians ironically replied that they subscribed all the more willingly to these formulas, since they could all be understood in the Arian sense. For his part, Eusebius of Caesarea tried to save Arius, calling for the acceptance of the *symbolon* which left the door open to equivocal expressions, but he received no support.

The more or less declared supporters of Arius used every dialectical resource at their disposal; but the deepest of Christian sentiments was against them. Beyond all the sophistries and arguments, one point remained as an indelible mark upon the very soul of Christianity, a point that the deacon Athanasius presented as the cornerstone: the indisputable fact of the redemption. Now the redemption has meaning only if God Himself becomes man, if

He Himself suffers, dies, and rises; if Christ is true God and true man at the same time. "And the Word was made flesh, and dwelt among us" (Jn 1:14). The affirmation of Saint John supposes that the *Logos* is fully God and not a man divinised according to the pagan idea. The Son is not a creature; He has always existed; He has always been at the right hand of the Father, united to Him, distinct but inseparable; He has always been infallible and perfect. The Council, under the influence of Athanasius, adopted the term *homoousios*, which was translated into Latin as *consubstantialem*.

The adoption of this term to affirm the perfect equality of the Word and the Father has remained fundamental for the Church to our own days. For a few days the Council Fathers hesitated about the need to promulgate a new *symbolon* which would more precisely express the old "Symbol of the Apostles" in use in the primitive Church; some thought it would be useless, that there was no need to try too hard to fix the terms of the mysteries and that it was better to adhere to the formulas of the past. But in the end, it was decided to proceed with the writing of this symbol of the orthodox faith. A new "rule of faith" was fixed, which was not substantially different from the one the first Christians had followed — the old "Symbol of the Apostles" — but which was more explicit, written in such a way that error could no longer be introduced. This text is the "Symbol of Nicea" which is recited on Sundays at Mass when, in the presence of the assembly of the faithful, its exact and subtle affirmations resound: *genitum non factum, consubstantialem Patri* — "begotten not made, consubstantial with the Father".

The merit of the theologians of the fourth century is that they fought unswervingly to safeguard the divinity of Christ which is the linchpin of Christianity. Each of the details of the Nicene formula aimed at averting a threat of heresy. Arius was thus condemned. The overwhelming majority affirmed that the Son is truly God, consubstantial with the Father. Only five bishops initially refused to sign this declaration, but after the emperor announced that he would use force to make them accept it, three gave in and only two preferred to be exiled with Arius in the mountains of Illyria.

The Council of Nicea closed a month later, in an atmosphere of triumph, on 25 August 325. The Arian question seemed to be closed forever. The conclusion of the Council coincided with the twentieth anniversary of the advent of Constantine's *imperium*, and he offered a sumptuous banquet for all the prelates, during which he gave a long speech in which he praised the results of the Council, invited each one present to maintain peace within himself, and to avoid all jealousy and discord. He also likened his own office to that of "a bishop on the outside". Then, fortified with letters from the emperor to their faithful as well as many gifts, the delegates departed. "God wanted," Constantine said, "the splendour of truth to triumph over dissensions, schisms, trouble, and the deadly poisons of discord."

The Council Fathers had just left when three of them, including Eusebius of Nicomedia, withdrew their signatures. The matter was ready to resurface. A certain number of Eastern theologians, including some who were perfectly orthodox, were close to thinking that the famous term "consubstantial" exaggerated the relations between the Father and the Son and gave certain advantages to the Modalists and Sabellians who wanted to see the Son only as a manifestation, a "modality" of the Father and not as a distinct person.

The dogma of the Incarnation of the Word was attacked from every side. In the gap between the intransigent "party" of Athanasius and that of the Arians, a "third party" was established: the "Semi-Arians", who in turn divided into the sects of the Anomoeans, the Homoeans and the Homoiousians, who recognised a certain analogy between the Father and the Son but denied that he was "begotten, not made, of the same substance as the Father", as the Nicene Creed declared. While the orthodox affirmed: "Christ is not a creature!" the non-orthodox added treacherous words: "a creature like the others…" They thought that by a seemingly insignificant textual change their doctrines could survive: they replaced the word *homoousios*, which means "of the same substance", with the term *homoiousios*, which means "of a similar substance". There is only a tiny difference between these two words, but this apparently insignificant difference was fundamental, and its importance should not be ignored. There is an abyss of difference in meaning between *homoousios* and *homoiousios*: the former means identification with God, while the latter means only a resemblance or a simple non-dissimilarity.

The defenders of the orthodox faith like Athanasius were accused of digging their heels in over mere words, of being intolerant fanatics. The party of the innovators would launch a war against them with no quarter; a war which Saint Basil and the Christian historian Socrates of Constantinople compared to furious "battles of the night".

The heretics, both Arian and Semi-Arian, had understood that their success would be dependent on two factors: the first was to remain within the Church, while the second was to obtain the support of political power and thus of Constantine, and then of his successors. This is in fact what happened, but their success was short-lived.

If the Church was able to survive such an ordeal, if in the end she came out not only intact but even strengthened, Daniel-Rops concludes, she owed it to a tiny legion of champions of the faith which at that time she had the good fortune to possess. Our attention is drawn to these great men consecrated to God rather than to the petty disputes into which heresy crumbles. They were passionately attached to the true faith, firm in their positions like rocks, men whom nothing could sway: neither intrigue nor threats nor exile nor prison. Two members of this noble army hold a place of first importance: Saint Athanasius and Saint Hilary of Poitiers.

4. The battle of Saint Athanasius

II THE CRISIS OF THE FOURTH CENTURY

Saint Athanasius is a personality who dominates the religious history of the East during those troubled years. Daniel-Rops describes him thus:

> "An extraordinarily penetrating intelligence, aware of all the subtleties of the Eastern spirit, but capable of grasping its false appearances and avoiding its pitfalls, thanks to a positive good sense that was never the laughing stock of anyone. A marvellously tempered character, of the same steel with which a short time before God had made his apostles and martyrs, agile and strong at the same time, upright in his intentions, skilful in his manoeuvres. Furthermore, a deeply religious soul, one of those great mystics for whom action is the effect of a prolonged prayer, one of those mystics who in the midst of the worst struggles never forgets that he is God's. He was sometimes said to be without measure, hateful in his fanaticism, ready to ignite violence and dispute around him: but this was a slander of his adversaries. Without a doubt, it cannot be said that a man of this world should use moderation at a time in which everything that nourished the Christian soul was being questioned, and which was a matter of life or death for the Church. But if the phrase of Saint Epiphanius is often quoted: 'He persuaded and exhorted, but if he was resisted, he used violence,' one also needs to remember these words, so full of true Christian charity, which Athanasius himself wrote: 'It is proper to religion not to compel but to convince.'"

Born in Alexandria around the year 300, Athanasius came to the fore as a close collaborator of his bishop Alexander at the Council of Nicea. When Alexander died in 328, his disciple Athanasius ascended to the episcopal chair. He remained bishop of Alexandria until his death, that is, for 45 years.

There was perhaps never such a troubled episcopal reign in the entire history of Christianity. The difficulties began the day after his consecration. All those whom Athanasius had fought against at Nicea allied themselves against the young bishop: from the Arian radicals to the Semi-Arian partisans of the two Eusebiuses, there were many who did not support the public role of Athanasius, to whom the *cathedra* of Alexandria gave strength and prestige. These grudges led to a new Council, held in Tyre in 335, in which the partisans of Eusebius laid an ambush for Athanasius. They accused him of having one of the schismatics killed, but the man who was allegedly dead reappeared, confounding the accusers. They accused him of imprudence and immorality, but the woman whom they had paid to give false testimony did not even recognise him and, instead, mistakenly accused another bishop of immoral relations with her! An organised lobby, however, existed against Athanasius. He went to Constantinople to denounce the Arian intrigues, but Constantine took him for an agitator capable of disturbing unity, and so Athanasius was deposed and ordered to depart for Trier. This first exile would be followed by another four. Recalled from exile in 337, he was attacked once again and forced to take refuge in Rome.

Athanasius was harshly persecuted by his own confrères and between 336 and 366 he was forced five times to abandon the city where he was bishop, spending long years in exile and in strenuous battles in defence of the faith, without any care for his own difficulties and worries. "They are only passing clouds!" he used to say with a smile.

In 341, just as a council of fifty bishops in Rome proclaimed Athanasius's innocence, the great Council of the Dedication in Antioch, which counted more than ninety bishops present, ratified

II THE CRISIS OF THE FOURTH CENTURY

the acts of the synods of Caesarea and Tyre and placed an Arian on his episcopal throne.

In 346, Athanasius finally returned to Alexandria, and for ten years he was able to enjoy sufficient tranquility there to carry out a vast correspondence with more than 400 bishops who were faithful to the dogma of Nicea and to write his doctrinal works which are most worthy of consideration. Meanwhile, however, two Semi-Arian bishops, Basil of Ancyra and Acacius of Caesarea, succeeded in entering into the good graces of the emperor. Under the influence of these counsellors, Constans, the sole master of the empire after the death of his brothers, sponsored an ever-growing number of councils in Italy and Gaul that were intended to destroy the doctrine of those orthodox bishops who were contemptuously called "Nicene".

It was the worst moment of Arian confusion. Pope Liberius himself (352–366), the successor of Julius I, faltered. The Council of Sirmium in 351 sought a middle ground between Catholic orthodoxy and Arianism. In the Council of Arles in 353 the Fathers, including Liberius's legate, signed a new condemnation of Athanasius. The bishops were forced to choose between condemning Athanasius and going into exile. Saint Paulinus (300–358), the bishop of Trier, was almost the only one who fought for the Nicene faith and was exiled to Phrygia, where he died following mistreatment at the hands of the Arians. Two years later, at the Council of Milan (355), more than thirty Western bishops signed the condemnation of Athanasius, and another orthodox father, Saint Hilary of Poitiers, was banished to Phrygia for his intransigent fidelity to orthodoxy.

In 357 Pope Liberius, overcome by the sufferings of exile and the insistence of his friends, but also driven by the "love of peace", signed the Semi-Arian formula of Sirmium and broke communion with Saint Athanasius, declaring him to be separated from the Roman Church because of his use of the term "consubstantial", as four letters handed down to us by Saint Hilary testify. Under the pontificate of Liberius, the Councils of Rimini (359) and Seleucia (359), which together constituted one great Council representing West and East, abandoned the term "consubstantial" of Nicea and established an equivocal *via media* between the Arians and Saint Athanasius. It seemed that rampant heresy had triumphed in the Church. "A dark, sad, and gloomy night spreads over the Church, as the lights of the world placed by God to illuminate the souls of the peoples have been exiled," wrote Saint Basil of Caesarea.

The twin Councils of Seleucia and Rimini, convoked by the emperor and envisaged as ecumenical like the Council of Nicea, are not numbered by the Church today among the eight ancient Ecumenical Councils. However, they included up to 560 bishops, almost all of the Fathers of Christianity, and they seemed to be "ecumenical" to their contemporaries. It was of this time that Saint Jerome coined the expression: "The whole world groaned and was astonished to find itself Arian".

Forced into hiding, Saint Athanasius fled into the desert, where he arrived at just the right moment to receive the last breath of his old friend Saint Anthony the Great, hermit and abbot of the Egyptian Thebaid. For six years Athanasius was the "invisible patriarch" who continued to direct his Church from afar, although the emissaries of the emperor persecuted him unceasingly. His polemical writings, in which Arianism and its byproducts were denounced, circulated everywhere. When finally with the death of Constans he could return to Alexandria, the Council that he called there sealed his triumph. All the confessors of the faith were there, proclaiming their unbending attachment to the dogma of Nicea, to the Son who is equal to the Father.

When he died in 373 he was the most celebrated man and the most eminent authority in the entire Church. Just a few years after his death, the great bishop of Constantinople, Gregory Nazianzen, celebrated him as "the pillar of the Church". In the same years, another emperor, the Arian Valens, not only fiercely persecuted the orthodox faith within the empire but also injected Arianism into the barbarian peoples who pressed on its borders. Under the illusion of more closely tying them to Byzantium, he sent Arian missionaries to the Goths and converted them to heresy. Valens however was defeated and killed by the Visigoths in the Battle of Adrianople in 378, which marked the beginning of the progressive decline of the Roman Empire.

Even though he led such a troubled existence, Saint Athanasius, Father of the Church, somehow found a way to leave an immense corpus of literary works, not only polemical but also dogmatic, like his discourses *Against the Greeks* and *On the Incarnation of the Word*, exegetical works like his *Exposition and Commentary on the Psalms*, moral works like his treatise *On Virginity*, and historical works like his *Life of Saint Anthony*, the first treatise about monastic life.

In the East the three Cappadocian Fathers followed the example of Athanasius: Basil of Caesarea, Gregory Nazianzen and Gregory of Nyssa, the brother of Basil. In the West two other great saints followed him: Eusebius of Vercelli and Hilary of Poitiers.

5. Saint Hilary of Poitiers, the Athanasius of the West

Saint Hilary of Poitiers (c.310–367) has entered into history as "the Athanasius of the West". And this is an accurate way to define his work and emphasise that the foundations of his thought are the same as those of the great Alexandrian Doctor. Like Athanasius, the saint of Gaul was moved by a passionate love for the Word Incarnate and consecrated his life to the defence of belief in the divinity of Jesus Christ.

Hilary was born around 310 in Poitiers to a wealthy pagan family, which imparted to him a solid education. As an adolescent — he himself relates the fact — he was struck by the Prologue of the Gospel of Saint John. As a young man habituated to spiritual things, he meditated at length on the famous phrase: *Et Verbum caro factum est et habitavit in nobis* — "And the Word was made flesh, and dwelt among us" (Jn 1:14). It was the means God used to conquer his soul. Some years later, when he was already married and had a daughter, Hilary was baptised. He then renounced matrimony and asked to enter holy orders. In 354 he became the bishop of his native city.

It was the height of the Arian battle. It seemed that heresy was triumphing. Hilary called for a synod in Paris in 355 in which Arianism was rejected. The champion of the Arian sect in Gaul, Saturninus of Arles, called a counter-synod which was held at Béziers, in the south of France. Hilary, rousing himself with all his strength against error, attracted to himself the lightning bolts of the pro-Arian Emperor Constans. He was sent to the opposite end of the empire and was forced to settle in Phrygia, in modern Turkey.

The stay was profitable. While he was directing his diocese by letter, he studied Eastern theology in depth, which the West knew poorly, and he began the drafting of his great dogmatic work against the Arians: *The Trinity*. In this moment he sought to bring the "homoiousians", who were the most moderate among the Arian heretics, back to Catholicism. His prestige in all the East became so great that the emperor judged it more prudent to send him back to Gaul. This act of clemency did not prevent Saint Hilary from issuing a pamphlet against the sovereign, friend of heretics, which would clandestinely make its way through the empire. Returning to Poitiers, he again took up the battle: in Paris, where the Council of 361 was a prelude to the Council of Alexandria that had to be convened by Saint Athanasius; in Italy, where all the Arians had such fear of his coming that they formed a league to lobby for his exile. At the same time, he worked in Gaul to spread the monastic ideal: he multiplied his visits to churches; he wrote dogmatic treatises and commentaries *On the Book of Job, On the Psalms, On Saint Matthew*, and a *Treatise on the Mysteries* in which he studied the prophetic figures of the Old Testament. Like Athanasius, Hilary demonstrated enormous, amazing activity. When he died in 367 all of Gaul considered him a saint. In 1851 Blessed Pius IX proclaimed him Doctor of the Church.

Only the Council of Constantinople, convened by Emperor Theodosius the Great in 381 under Pope Saint Damasus (367–384), marked the end of Arianism in the empire. At the Council, the *symbolon* of Nicea was reconfirmed almost to the letter, and it was defined that the Holy Ghost "proceeds from the Father, and with the Father and the Son is adored and glorified". Thanks to Emperor Theodosius, Christianity was declared the State religion, and the work begun with the victory of Constantine at Saxa Rubra on 28 October 312 could be said to truly be complete.

The sixty years between the Council of Nicea and the Council of Constantinople were years of bewilderment, confusion, and a drama of conscience in which Catholics wondered where the Church was. Cardinal Newman wrote in his book *The Arians of the Fourth Century* that in the age of the Arian crisis "it was the Christian people who, under the protection of Providence, constituted the strength of Athanasius, Hilary, Eusebius of Vercelli and other great and solitary confessors who would have faltered without their help."

Saint Hilary writes in this period that the ears of the faithful who interpreted the equivocal affirmations of the Semi-Arian theologians in an orthodox sense were holier than the hearts of their priests. Hilary, writes Dom Guéranger, had to fight against the timid men of the Church, who had become incapable of grasping the supernatural essence of the Mystical Body of Christ, since naturalism had distorted their spirit.

The Church, however, in the midst of storms, never loses her attributes which always make her one, even when she appears to be divided and fragmented; holy, even when the faults of her pastors defile her; Catholic, that is, universal, even when she seems to lose the certainty of her own salvific uniqueness and addresses only one part of the believers in the world; apostolic, even when disputes arise between the successors of the apostles. She in fact enjoys the promise of indefectibility in her action of defending and preaching the faith, of the administration of the sacraments and the governance of the faithful, and in times of crisis great champions of the faith like Saint Athanasius and Saint Hilary rise up to remind her of these truths.

Today too the Church is living through a very grave and difficult situation, and not only because of the persecutions to which Christians are being subjected in every part of the world, but also and above all because she appears to be suffering and weakened as at the time of the Arian crisis and many other crises of the Church. It was Benedict XVI himself who recalled this by applying to our times the metaphor used by Saint Basil to describe the years following the Council of Nicea: a nocturnal battle in a stormy sea.

Nothing worse could be imagined for the barque of the Church than the situation recalled by the pope who, not by chance, decided to announce that 2012 would be the Year of Faith.

For our part, we imitate Saint Athanasius and all the saints, including the unknown ones, who raised the torch of faith in the fourth century, even at the cost of being called fanatical and intransigent, and we ask for their protection, and also that of the Blessed Mother, *Auxilium Christianorum*, in order to face the trials to come.

Radio Maria, 19 October 2011

II THE CRISIS OF THE FOURTH CENTURY

CHAPTER III

The monks conquer the world

1. Monasticism as a category of the Christian spirit

The first three centuries of the life of the Church were an age of suffering and persecutions in which Christians responded generously to the words of the Gospel: "If any man will come after me, let him deny himself, and take up his cross daily, and follow me" (Lk 9:23), and also "You shall be brought before governors, and before kings for my sake, for a testimony to them and to the Gentiles" (Mt 10:18).

The first Christians did not hesitate to follow this path. They witnessed to the truth even to the shedding of their blood. The Church gave this testimony the name of martyrdom. The age of persecutions was also called the age of the martyrs because almost all the popes of the first centuries and a great part of the bishops and priests sealed their faith with martyrdom. The way of martyrdom, however, was not an isolated moment in the history of the Church, but a model which countless Christians would follow over the centuries, who like their fellow believers of the first centuries would be ready to offer their lives to give witness to Christ, the only Way, Truth, and Life (Jn 14:6).

We have seen, however, that the fourth century saw an important shift in the history of the Church, known as the "Constantinian shift": the battle of the Milvian Bridge, in which the army of Constantine, fighting under the banner of the cross, defeated the pagan army of Maxentius, and the subsequent Edict of Milan with which the new emperor granted full liberty to Christians in the year 313.

The Constantinian shift, which marked the reconciliation between Christianity and the empire, has often been accused of being a betrayal of evangelical ideals and of compromising Christians with power. How many times have we heard it said that there is a need to purify our faith from the incrustations and hangovers of the Constantinian era in order to return to the origins of our faith, to the purity of the primitive Church! That these accusations are false is demonstrated by the fact that in the fourth century, precisely in parallel with the so-called Constantinian shift, and in harmony with it, a new phenomenon developed characterised by the Christian rejection of the world and of every form of power. We are speaking, of course, of monasticism.

How, one might ask, can two apparently opposing objectives be reconciled: the social conquest of the world after Constantine — that is, its Christianisation — and the flight from the world undertaken by the monks in this same period? In order to understand this, we must turn to the words of the Gospel: "My kingdom is not of this world" (Jn 18:36). This is not to say that the Kingdom of God does not extend to the world and is not fulfilled in the world, but only that it does not have its origin or its final end (both supernatural) in this world. The Christian lives in the world, and the Christian must conquer the world. The conquest of the world, its Christianisation, can take place through different means: monasticism is one of these means, martyrdom another and the Crusades would become one later: they are ideal models destined to span the centuries, not opposed to one another but complementary, arising from the same spirit of faith.

In order to understand in depth what monasticism is, it is necessary to understand the true nature of Christianity and the Church. Monasticism in fact is nothing other than a form of complete dedication to God by means of the faithful observance of the three evangelical counsels: the renunciation of material goods (poverty), the renunciation of the pleasures of the body and the joys of the family (celibacy) and the renunciation of one's own independence (obedience). Jesus sanctifies marriage but also says: "And every one that hath left house, or brethren, or sisters, or father, or mother, or wife, or children, or lands for my name's sake, shall receive an hundredfold, and shall possess life everlasting" (Mt 19:29).

Private property is legitimised by two commandments of the Decalogue, but Jesus says: "If thou wilt be perfect, go sell what thou hast, and give to the poor, and thou shalt have treasure in heaven: and come follow me" (Mt 19:21).

These renunciations are a free choice, because they are counsels and not commandments of the Lord. They are not an order but advice, not for all but to some. In a word, it is a vocation offered by the Lord, an appeal which has since resounded through all the centuries. Error, and even heresy, begins when one pretends to transform the evangelical counsels into obligatory commands for everyone. For example, there was the idea of a Church of "the holy" or "the pure" opposed to the Church of "sinners". This inspired the first heresies of Marcion, Montanus and Donatus which characterise the secular religions of the twentieth century like communism, imposing the sharing of goods by decree, denying the natural right to private property.

The institution of monasticism dates to the third and fourth century, but the search for forms of Christian perfection began in the Church from the very first years of her history. The characteristic of those who wanted to apply the evangelical counsels was, from the beginning, the choice to embrace the state of virginity to signify one's separation from the world. Virginity, however, before being a physical condition, is a moral choice. The first model that we have of religious life is in fact Saint Mary Magdalene, the repentant sinner who after the Lord's death left Palestine with a few companions and landed miraculously in Provence, dedicating herself for thirty years to the eremitical life in silence and prayer. These were the years in which the apostles were spreading the Gospel to every corner of the earth and sealing their testimony with martyrdom. Saint Mary Magdalene accompanied their evangelical action with her penance and prayers.

2. Monasticism in the East

The first form of monasticism was called eremitical (from *eremos* — a desert place) or solitary (whence *monakhos*, from *monos* — alone) to indicate a type of life separated from men and entirely directed to God. This was also an effect of the persecutions. From the life of Saint Paul of Thebes written by Saint Jerome we know that the future hermit took refuge in the mountains in order to flee persecution. Saint Jerome was among the first to use the term "anchorite" in the sense of "one who lives in desert places" (Epistle 22, 36). God is not encountered in noise but in silence and meditation. Two degrees were distinguished in anchoritism: some led an entirely solitary life; others instead, although dwelling in separate cells, formed a sort of colony around a church in which they would gather for common prayer. Egypt was considered the archetypal land of early monasticism. Centres of Egyptian eremitical life were found in the desert of Nitria and the desert of Scetis, south of Alexandria. In order to understand the mentality of the Egyptian monks, so different from that of our time, it is wonderful to read the *Apophtegmata Patrum (Sayings of the Desert Fathers)*, a series of sentences attributed to the oral teaching of the Fathers of the desert.

Saint Anthony the Great (c.251–356) is considered the founder of the anchoritic life. His life was written in 357 by Saint Athanasius, who knew him personally and was supported and counselled by him in his battle against Arianism. The *Life of Saint Anthony* was translated into Latin and exercised a notable influence on the spread and formation of monasticism in the West. Anthony was born in 251 and died in 356 at the age of 105. Towards the end of the third century, he retired to the desert between the Nile and the Red Sea, and spent his life immersed in prayer and work. "He prayed continually," his biography records, "and remembered everything: for him his memory took the place of books." Like many hermits of that time, he was not a priest nor a cleric, but many disciples immediately gathered around him, attracted by his life of perfection, and thus eremitism spread, first in Upper Egypt and then also in Lower Egypt.

The form of monastic life instituted by Anthony was that of a hermit who separated himself from his peers and wanted to be in dialogue with God face to face. There was no organisation within eremitical life: if a monk stood out because of his holiness and wisdom, other monks allowed themselves to be led by him, and thus they gathered together in the environs of his cell, calling him their spiritual "father" or "abbot" (from *abbas, apa, amba*), but there was no official community properly speaking. However, it soon became apparent that many candidates for perfection could not withstand the dangers of absolute isolation and that it was possible to offer mutual support, while preserving the desire for solitude, in a reciprocal spirit of charity.

Thus there was a development from the eremitical life to the communal or cenobitic life. A first step towards this was taken simultaneously in Palestine and in Egypt. Another Egyptian saint, Pachomius (287–347), a former soldier of Constantine, began to live as a hermit following his conversion, but around 320 he founded the first monastery in the Thebaid (Upper Egypt), gathering together for the first time a group of monks who led a common life (*koinós bios*) under the authority of an abbot, wearing for the first time a monastic habit with a hood and a cincture made of leather. The monastery, an enclosure forbidden to laymen and especially to women, isolated the community from the world. A strict rule ordered the life of the monks and their time. Intellectual work went hand in hand with manual labour, while frequent conferences explained sacred scripture to the monks. Prayer was undertaken in common as well as in private. New communities, daughter houses of Pachomius's first foundation, sprang up all over Egypt. His sister Mary founded two convents for women. At the end of the fourth century his congregation counted no less than seven thousand monks.

In Palestine, where according to Saint Jerome, the first monk was Hilarion of Gaza, they began to call monasteries by the name of *laura* or *lauras*, which has remained the custom in Greek Orthodox Christianity. A *laura* (from the Greek word meaning "village") was a true village of monks who constructed a group of separate cells that were near each other, surrounded by a hedge or a wall. This fence created a boundary: it was a cloister separating those who were outside and a circle uniting those who were within. Saint Chariton, who lived as an ascetic near Jerusalem, is considered the founder of the *lauras* of Pharan, Donka (near Jericho) and Sonka (near Bethlehem). He and Saint Hilarion founded convents and hermitages throughout the great places whose names are found in sacred scripture.

Monasticism spread with amazing rapidity. In Mesopotamia, Eugenius, a former pearl fisher, a disciple of Pachomius, established a monastery on Mount Nisibis. Other shepherd monks are remembered who prayed to God on the borders of Arabia and Syria, in the solitude of the steppe in the midst of their wandering flocks. All of Asia Minor was infused with monasticism in a short time.

The true founder of Eastern monasticism is considered to be Saint Basil the Great (329–379), to whom is attributed a Rule that spread throughout the entire East and also in the West, and who became the bishop of Caesarea and metropolitan of Cappadocia in 370. Basil belonged to a deeply Christian family: he was the nephew of martyrs, the son of upper-class merchants who had left everything to flee from the pursuit of Diocletian, the brother of a foundress of convents (Saint Macrina) and of two other saints (Gregory of Nyssa and Peter of Sebastea). He was also a man of action, a great thinker, a talented administrator, and a fervent believer. Around the years 357–358, Basil made a long journey which took him to Egypt, Palestine, Syria, and Mesopotamia. Wherever he went, he gathered the experiences of the monks who populated those deserts. Upon returning to Asia Minor, he became a monk and set up a monastery with some companions in the region of Neo-Caesarea in Pontus, following the rule of Pachomius, with some modifications.

In his two writings on ascetical life in common (cenobitism), called the *Greater Monastic Rules* and the *Lesser Rules*, Pachomius summarises the ideal of cenobitism in these three points: a) the love of God and neighbour as a perfect expression of the law of charity; b) the study of sacred scripture understood as the highest manifestation of the will of God; c) the practice of the monastic life considered as a perfect form of renunciation of the world.

The reform of Saint Basil tends to limit the number of monks in every monastery so that the superior can better direct them; spiritually he insists greatly on the need to develop the virtues of humility, patience and charity in the conventual life. And he further had the idea of joining schools to monasteries, an idea that would have a decisive impact on the development of Christian civilisation. His rule has remained at the foundation of Eastern monasticism, just as his liturgy is at the foundation of the liturgies of the Eastern churches.

In the East many other forms of monasticism spread, such as the "stylites" and the "enclosed". The stylites made a vow to remain on columns that were from 3 to 18 meters high. Their pioneer was the Syrian Saint Simeon (c.390–459), called "the Stylite" because he spent 37 years living on a column near Antioch. After his death one of the largest basilicas in Syria was erected near this column.

The "enclosed" were so called because they had themselves walled up for a long time, or even permanently, inside a cell to dedicate themselves fully to contemplation, reading, and manual labour. The Council of Trullo established that no one could take up this way of life unless they had first spent at least three years in a monastery, but once they were enclosed they could no longer leave their cell. After a period of great success, this form of monasticism would decline; but at Mount Athos on the Chalkidiki peninsula recluses may still be seen who spend their existence in absolute solitude as prisoners of God. Today choosing such a state of life may seem bizarre, but they were not going against nature: they took the principle of renouncing the world to gain eternal life to its logical conclusion. In fact, certain forms of modern life would have appeared to these monks (as they should to us) more than bizarre — completely absurd — as they violate the laws of the nature and the Christian order.

During the fifth and sixth centuries, the number of monasteries continued to multiply and their popularity also increased. In 518 in Constantinople there were 607 monasteries of men and a great number of monasteries of women; they occupied vast territories, in particular along the Sea of Marmara where the famous monastery of Studios was built, noted for its fidelity to the See of Rome during the Acacian Schism, and which became the seat of the Acemites, the "insomniacs", founded in 405 by the monk Alexander. They led a common life and, subdivided into various choirs, they dedicated themselves uninterruptedly to the divine office, even at night (hence their name).

The Council of Chalcedon juridically defined monasticism, placing monasteries under the jurisdiction of their respective diocesan bishops.

3. Monasticism in the West

It was thanks to Saint Athanasius that monasticism spread from the East. We have recalled the turbulent life of Saint Athanasius, the bishop of Alexandria, who was exiled to the West by the Arian emperors and opposed by the Semi-Arians because of his fidelity to orthodoxy. He went to Trier, one of the Western capitals of the empire, and in the middle of the fourth century also spent some time in Rome. Thus in a providential manner he made the extraordinary life of Saint Anthony and the Egyptian hermits known in the West, prompting Western Christians to follow their example. In Italy, the first centres of monasticism were Rome and Milan, thanks to two great Fathers of the Church, Saint Jerome and Saint Ambrose. In Rome, a group of aristocratic women gathered under the guidance of Jerome to lead a more perfect life founded on prayer and virginity, following his appeal to the new Christian nobility. Among these women we remember Saint Marcella, who made her palace on the Aventine Hill into a sort of convent for women, including Fabiola, Proba, and Paula — all of whom were raised to the altars. "The patrician phalanx," Dom Guéranger recalls, "constituted the best part of the monastic army, at its birth in the West, and forever communicated its character of ancient greatness, but in its ranks, with a title equal to that of fathers and brothers, were the virgins and widows, and sometimes brides along with their spouse. Marcella was the first to obtain direction from Jerome and it would be Marcella, despite her humility, who after her teacher had passed away would become the oracle consulted by everyone with any difficulty relating to the interpretation of scripture. Following Marcella there were: Furia, Fabiola, and Paula; names recalling great ancestors: the Camilli, the Fabii, the Scipioni." In Milan, Saint Ambrose founded a monastery near the city walls. In Vercelli, Saint Eusebius (†c.370) introduced the common life of clerics, and the same thing took place in Verona with the bishop Saint Zeno (362–372), as well as in Nola, where Saint Paulinus founded a monastery over the tomb of Saint Felix in 395.

III THE MONKS CONQUER THE WORLD

The fascination exerted by the fame of the hermits and monks who were residents in Egypt, Palestine and Syria led many Western Christians towards these lands. The Roman matron Saint Melania, who was widowed, went to Palestine in 378 and founded a monastery on the Mount of Olives. She was followed several decades later by her niece Melania, called "the Younger", who is also a saint. Jerome himself moved to Palestine in 386, followed by Paula and her daughter Eustochium. Two monasteries founded by him were built in Jerusalem: one for men, the other for women.

In Gaul, monasticism first sprang to life with Saint Martin (316–397), who was born in the lands of Pannonia and after serving in the Roman army became a hermit near Poitiers and a disciple of its bishop, Saint Hilary. We have recalled earlier the names of Saint Athanasius, bishop of Alexandria, and Eusebius, bishop of Vercelli. These men, along with Saint Hilary, the bishop of Poitiers, not only strenuously fought heresy, but were also great promoters of monasticism. Their apostolic action against heresy was born of a profound spirit of prayer. While previously in the East monks were not priests, Saint Martin established that a monk could also be a cleric. At his initiative the first monastery in Gaul was founded at Ligugé. Later when he became a bishop the saint wanted to preserve his monastic life and he had the abbey of Marmoutier built in the vicinity of Tours. Martin sought to reconcile his pastoral duties with the monastic life which he nurtured in Gaul, Spain, and Britain. He evangelised a great part of Gaul and was considered the protector of the Franks. He died in 397 and at his death two thousand monks attended his funeral. The shrine built over his tomb was the most revered in all of Gaul.

In the year 410, a monastery which was destined to have a great influence was founded in southern Gaul, on one of the islands of Lérins near the city of Cannes, by Saint Honoratus (†429), who was later the bishop of Arles. From this monastery came Saint Vincent of Lérins, Salvianus of Marseilles, and Saint Caesarius (470–542), bishop of Arles, to whom is attributed the first two monastic rules typical of Gaul: one directed to monks and the other to "holy virgins", which was adopted by Saint Radegunda in Poitiers (560). At the end of the fifth century there were 40 monasteries in Gaul, and by the year 600 there were 240.

The figure of Saint John Cassian (c.360–435) should also be recalled as a bridge between Eastern and Western monasticism. He was a Scythian monk from Dobruja (the region between the Danube and the Black Sea, modern Romania and Bulgaria) who founded two monasteries in Marseilles, one for men and the other for women, and authored even before Saint Benedict a Western monastic rule. Among his works which have come down to us are the *Monastic Institutions* published in 417–418, which influenced the Rule of Saint Benedict.

In Africa, the monastic ideal was spread by Saint Augustine, who had experienced it in Milan and Rome, but he developed it with his own particular vision. He gathered members of the clergy around himself in order to lead an ascetical life together with them. The Rule of Saint Augustine, written around the year 400, may be considered the most ancient of the Latin monastic rules. Augustine also oversaw the establishment of monasteries of virgins. In Hippo, his sister was the superior. His *Letter 211* sent to the nuns of Hippo was the basis for many subsequent religious orders.

4. Saint Benedict of Nursia

Monasticism asserted itself powerfully in the history of the Church from the fourth century when, we may say, the age of martyrs was succeeded by the age of monks. The new institution was welcomed by all Christians with the greatest favour. For three centuries the model of perfection had been epitomised by the martyrs whose relics were venerated and whose deeds were read aloud. Now that the era of persecutions was drawing to a close, a new ideal of perfection arose, that of the monks who also led extraordinary lives and to whom, as to the martyrs, great miracles were attributed. The wind of the Holy Ghost never ceased to assist the Church but it blew in new ways.

It is true that there was no lack of resistance to the new form of life, which was condemned as too extreme and intransigent by the pagans and by Christians who were more moderate or worldly. Even some bishops harboured a certain mistrust of a way of life that seemed excessive to them or that, perhaps because of its austerity, seemed to constitute a critique of the bland Christianity of the majority of the clergy. In cities like Milan and Carthage there were strong anti-monastic reactions. Some bishops sought to discourage the new movement, ever more widespread and powerful, but which appeared to them to be too independent of the authority of the bishops and disturbing because of the new fervour of life it spread.

The institution of monasticism marked an important stage in the development of Christianity. Daniel-Rops recalls how the practice of the "examination of conscience", which Saint Augustine greatly praised, is owed in large part to the writings of the Desert Fathers, and above all to Saint Anthony the Great. It was the monks who initiated the practice of giving spiritual direction to souls. From the monasteries came the idea of the transferability of merits: the prayer of the cloisters benefits all of humanity. Saint Macarius, the monk of Egypt, exclaimed: "Happy the monk who considers with joy the progress and salvation of all men as his own!" When the martyrs were no longer there to redeem human misery, the monks by their prayers replaced them in that office which the French writer Huysmans defined with a vivid and precise expression as "God's lightning rods".

In terms of history, the monasteries would play another equally crucial role. When the storm of the barbarians was unleashed, the monasteries would provide many bishops who were destined to be the bastions of the Church and of society. It would be they who, in the schools and workshops of the copyists, would safeguard civilisation in the midst of the worst cataclysms. It is thanks to these men and women, providentially inserted into the new institution of monasticism, that the uninterrupted celebration of the Holy Sacrifice of the Mass and the Divine Office continued. The crowning glory of this era is found in an extraordinary figure: Saint Benedict, the father of the Christian civilisation which established itself on the ruins of the Roman one.

Saint Benedict was born around 480 in Umbria, in the town of Norcia, or Nursia, to a patrician Roman family, and he ended his earthly existence at Montecassino on 21 March 543. His life was tied to three places: Nursia, his birthplace; Subiaco, where he had his most intense religious experience; and Montecassino, the place where he died and where he built a monastery destined to enter into European history.

Saint Benedict spent three years as a hermit in Subiaco, in the valley of the Aniene River, in a cave that today is known as the *Sacro Speco* or "Holy Cave". Only after having tamed his flesh and overcome spiritual temptations did he decide to leave this refuge in order to found the first monasteries under a new rule. The abbey of Montecassino, the most famous monastery in all of Christianity, was founded in 529 on a mountain halfway between Rome and Naples, where there were still pagan temples. Saint Benedict destroyed these temples and established the first monastic community in the West. The foundation of this abbey represented the birth of Christian Europe which began to take shape after the fall of the Roman Empire.

Describing Saint Benedict's mission in his homily *Exultent Hodie* of 18 September 1947, Pius XII affirmed that:

"He was a giant who opened new paths for a misguided age. Filled with the same spirit as all of the just, as Saint Gregory the Great says, he distinguished himself by love for God and neighbour; he was grave and serene; he had a great influence over all; he mastered himself and was adorned with angelic habits, distinguished for his gift of prophecy and miracles; a new Abraham, he generated a family of religious men; a new Moses, he established a law and led the people to sacrifice in the desert."

The law that Benedict established is the famous *Regula Monachorum* ("Rule of Monks"), which not only summarises his person and his work, but also constitutes one of the foundations of all western spirituality. The great merit of the Rule is above all that of having known how to harmonise and blend together the preceding monastic rules, adapting them in an admirable way to the needs and habits of the peoples of the West.

The Rule consists of 73 chapters of different lengths, and it has come down to us in three versions. The Prologue and the first chapters (I-VIII) lay down the foundations of the cenobitic life; the chapters immediately following (IX-XVIII) dictate the norms of liturgical life and life in common; they define the spirit that must animate both communal life as well as private prayer; and they establish the order of the life of the abbey and regulate its daily routine.

The Rule, a "small compendium of the Gospel", as it has been defined, was the benchmark of monasticism, the model for all rules that would discipline all forms of religious life subsequent to the Benedictine model. Its fundamental characteristic was the common life of the monks, who formed a great family.

The Benedictine monastery was a social organism governed by the authority of the abbot, similar to a *pater familiae*, with broad powers who combines loving severity with *discretio*, the ability to understand the attitudes and weaknesses of the individual monks. In addition to the three traditional vows of poverty, chastity and obedience, they made a vow of stability "of place" (*stabilitas loci*) to which the monk ties himself at the time at which he enters the monastery.

In the Middle Ages the so-called mendicant orders would arise, characterised by an apparent instability due to the continuous movement that saw them travelling the streets of Europe from one monastery to another. But it was a historical moment in which stability was the general rule of society. Medieval civilisation was an ordered society, within which movement was possible as an expression of vitality, not of disorder. The age of Saint Benedict was by contrast an era of great chaos. The *stabilitas loci* of the monks constituted an element of stability that was spiritual and moral even before it was physical. The monasteries were thus the stabilising element of a society that was now lacking order and a centre.

The principal duty of the monk was the *opus Dei*, the Divine Office, to which everything else was subordinate: reading, study and manual labour carried out both in the fields and inside the monastery. The centre of the life of the monk was the liturgy, celebrated day and night in common at fixed times. But the great novelty of Saint Benedict, in comparison to Eastern monasticism, was that of having work, both intellectual work and manual labour, united to prayer. *Ora et labora* (pray and work) is the formula that summarises the Benedictine ideal. Starting from prayer, the work flows out and then returns. It is not a question of contrasting prayer and work but of affirming the primacy of prayer over works. This teaching is valid above all in an era like our own, characterised by a feverish and unceasing activity without the deep breath of prayer over men's works. The historian Giorgio Falco writes: "This therefore is the existence of the monk: praying, reading, and working. Everything is disciplined: the calendar and the daily *horarium*, the liturgy, study, work, the quantity of eating and drinking, the service of the kitchen and the laundry."

Modern man is immersed in the din of exterior works and forgets the gaze lifted up to God, the *opus Dei*, which gives the only possible meaning to his life. The monastic community is conceived under two aspects, which merge into one and have as a common principle love of one's fellow man and love of God. In the monastery the horizontal relationship to one's fellow man is based on the vertical relationship with God. As John Paul II affirmed: "Love pervades and inspires everything, as in every true and healthy family: it is enough to recall that testament of charity that is chapter 72 of the *Rule*" (Address to the faithful of Cassino, 20 September 1980).

On 24 October 1964, Saint Benedict was proclaimed the patron of Europe by Paul VI. When he died in 543, his work had led to the founding of three monasteries: Montecassino, Subiaco and Terracina. A century later there were more than one hundred Benedictine communities.

According to Daniel-Rops, the proliferation of monasteries is the most important fact of the history of the medieval Church. Beginning in the sixth century, and for many generations thereafter, kings and bishops, the influential and the wealthy, would all compete to contribute to their foundation. The communities counted an average of two hundred men each, coming from every social class.

Abbeys for women also multiplied, to the point of having abbesses who had jurisdiction over double monasteries, one male and one female, and they were obeyed perfectly. The works carried out in the lands next to the abbeys were impressive: the clearing of lands that had remained uncultivated since the fall of the empire and the barbarian invasions, the reclaiming of unsanitary land, the intelligent cultivation of fields, and large livestock farms. Hamlets, villages, and cities formed around the monastic centres. Roads, bridges, and canals multiplied, while hospitals, guesthouses, and large amounts of alms donated to the needy met the needs of the time. The income of the monasteries was not only used for the support of the communities and the embellishment of the buildings, but also for works of charity, above all hospitals and guesthouses for pilgrims.

The intellectual influence of the monasteries was no less profound. From the very beginning the monasteries had their schools and their *scriptoria*, rooms for copying and transcribing the codices in which the patient work of the scribes multiplied the number of books, enabling them to be more widely known and studied. The office of copyist required great commitment and sacrifice: *Si tres digiti scribunt, totum corpus laborat*, declared the scribe of Cassino — "three fingers write, but the whole body labours". The codices and texts, guarded jealously by the monks in the libraries, contributed to saving the cultural patrimony of the ancient world.

5. The spread of the Benedictine Rule

The large-scale dissemination of the Rule of Saint Benedict in the Western Church was a slow process that contributed significantly to the evangelisation of Europe. Outside of Italy, the first country where the Rule of Saint Benedict was known and adopted was England, where Saint Gregory the Great sent Saint Augustine of Canterbury as a missionary.

When Augustine arrived in England, monastic life was already flourishing. It had arrived in the British Isles more than a century earlier, and above all in Ireland, thanks to Saint Patrick (c.385–461).

England was then inhabited by the Britons, who had allied themselves with the Romans before the Romans had withdrawn their legions. Together they had fought against the Picts who lived in the northern part of the island. From this land came a heretic, Pelagius, who arriving in Rome spread his errors there as well. Precisely in order to fight Pelagianism, Saint Germanus of Auxerre (c.378–448) organised a missionary expedition to the British Isles in 432, accompanied by the young Patrick, sent there as a missionary by Pope Celestine I (422–432). Patrick worked in this land, obtaining extraordinary results, leaving a deep Catholic imprint that it would never lose over the centuries.

III THE MONKS CONQUER THE WORLD

In Ireland, from the year 444, the monastery of Armagh became the metropolitan see and the most important place in the ecclesial life of the nation. One of the characteristics of Irish monasticism was its missionary zeal and its capacity for expansion. Around the year 591, Saint Columbanus (c.543–615) departed from Bangor (near Belfast), the most famous of his monasteries, and went to Gaul where he founded the monastery of Luxeuil. He then went on to the Vosges. Columbanus had an unyielding character and imposed privations and mortifications of every sort upon himself. Forced into exile, he departed for Italy with twelve companions, including Gallus (550–645), who fell ill along the way, and founded the monastery of Saint Gallen, in modern Switzerland. Columbanus continued on, overcoming every difficulty, until he reached the Trebbia River, near Piacenza, where he founded his last monastery in Bobbio, and where he died in 615. The monasteries founded by Columbanus and his disciples progressively adopted the Benedictine Rule, which during the Carolingian period, with the help of Saint Benedict of Aniane (c.750–821), was adopted by all the monasteries of the empire (*Capitulare Monasticum* of 817).

The birth of monasticism was an extraordinary phase in the history of Christianity. This movement was not only an exceptional instrument of personal sanctification, through the radical application of the evangelical counsels, it also elevated divine worship to incomparable heights. It had a profound influence on social and political life, because European civilisation was formed in the image of the monasteries, and animated by their spirit. For this reason, Pius XII called Saint Benedict "the father of Europe", affirming that "while the hordes of barbarians swept through the provinces, he who was called the last of the Romans, reconciling *Romanità* (if we may be permitted to use Tertullian's expression) and the Gospel, drew strong help from these sources to unite the peoples of Europe under the banner of the hope of Christ and to give a happy order to Christian society. In fact, from the North Sea to the Mediterranean, from the Atlantic Ocean to the Baltic Sea, legions of Benedictines spread out, who with the cross, books, and the plough tamed those rough and uncivilised people" (Homily *Exultent Hodie*, cit.).

"The Benedictines are the fathers of European civilisation," wrote Léo Moulin (1906–1996), recalling that even the laws of etiquette that we observe at table today (tablecloths, napkins, flowers, silence, cleanliness, the sequence of foods, mutual courtesy, a certain way of behaving) were invented by the monks who transformed food into a dish or — *pietanza* in Italian — that is, something linked to *piety*: food that is received and consumed with gratitude and respect.

Etiquette, courtesy, and civilised manners are all the fruit of Christian civilisation, and the contemporary barbarisation of customs is the result of the loss of the Christian spirit. This spirit, which finds one of its most elevated forms in the Benedictine spirit, is above all a spirit of prayer. This spirit of prayer, the Benedictine *opus Dei*, is the worship offered to God in the Holy Sacrifice of the Mass and the Divine Office. In order to give new impetus to this liturgical dimension, Pope Benedict XVI reaffirmed full citizenship to the traditional Mass in the ancient Roman rite with his Motu Proprio *Summorum Pontificum*. This same Mass offered by Saint Benedict and his monks, still celebrated in many Benedictine abbeys in France and Italy, is gradually returning and spreading throughout the whole Church, to the benefit of souls and to the greater glory of God.

Radio Maria, 16 November 2011

CHAPTER IV

Pagan Rome and Christian Rome

1. The barbarians at the end of the fourth century

Historical periods resemble one another: each is in some sense a prefiguration and image of the next. This is why it is worth dwelling upon a particular historical era of the Church: the fourth century, which is also the era in which the decline of the Roman Empire began. Benedict XVI in his Address to the Roman Curia on 20 December 2005 compared our own time to the era of the decline and fall of the Roman Empire, an institution that seemed immortal but which fell into ruin during the fourth and fifth centuries after Christ.

It did not all happen suddenly. A sense of foreboding began to spread towards the end of the fourth century: the awareness that a world was collapsing, that something had ended and could not be born again. This sentiment, as Henri Daniel-Rops observes, was expressed in a general malaise, which was not only psychological but also political, economic and social. There was no need to be a philosopher of history to see it.

The order, peace, and universality which characterised the past was nothing but a bitter memory. Even the humblest citizens felt that things were going badly, that they could not continue as they were: the dissolution of a society brings different crises with it that overlap and intertwine with each other, aggravating the situation and rendering it beyond repair. It was an economic crisis, a political crisis, and above all a moral crisis.

The effects of the economic crisis could be seen in inflation, in the black market, and in the debasement of currency, which was accompanied by heavy taxation. Among the reasons for this economic crisis was also, as in every era of decadence, a demographic decline. People did not bring children into the world, because they feared the future and because they were immersed in a climate of hedonism and relativism. Corruption and dishonesty ruled the day. The imperial courts were the centre of every sort of intrigue. As the fourth century Roman historian Ammianus Marcellinus wrote, "The palace is a seedbed of vices whose germs spread everywhere."

In was at this moment, Lactantius says, that the number of officials began to surpass the number of taxpayers. It was no longer possible to either work or travel without the permission of an inspector. Government agents stole and looted. No one knew whether the court of Milan, Trier, or Constantinople was really in command.

The Roman legions that formed the backbone of the empire were no longer the bastions of ancient virtues. There were no longer Romans in the Roman legions, because the exhausted citizens no longer wanted to fight or work. The conscripts cut off their thumbs, so they would not be able to shoot with the bow. The barbarians who migrated into the empire filled the empty places left by the citizens of Rome in labour camps and in the army.

In this decadent society, the barbarians appeared on the horizon as a new force and Rome viewed this new force with a mixture of fascination and fear.

The word "barbarian" was used to designate the peoples not subject to Roman dominion, in particular the Germanic peoples who settled on the borders of the empire and then invaded it in the fifth century.

The borders of the Roman Empire extended for 15,000 kilometres, defended by a kind of "iron curtain": the *limes* or *vallum*, a system of palisades, guard towers, and moats that were a marvel of military engineering. In the third century the Roman *limes* stretched from the Atlantic and the North Sea all the way to the Caspian Sea, and extended across Europe from the Rhine to the Danube,

IV PAGAN ROME AND CHRISTIAN ROME

Britain, North Africa, and Asia Minor all the way to Armenia and Mesopotamia.

On the borders of this immense empire were, to the east, the Parthians and Arabs; to the south, on African soil, Ethiopians, Libyans, and Berbers; to the north, the Germanic peoples who had not been conquered by the empire; while the Goths began to push from Scandinavia towards the Vistula. It must be added that in addition to the Roman world, centred around the Mediterranean, and the barbarian world on the borders of the empire, there was also a third domain, the Asian world, which pressed on the barbarians from the east. Savage hordes like the Huns appeared on the Don and the Dnieper and advanced towards the Danube. The difference between the barbarians of northern Europe and those who came from Asia was that the former were willing to assimilate, integrating themselves among the people they conquered, while the latter had a policy of destruction and extermination, reducing the conquered peoples to slavery.

The barbarian invasions did not arrive suddenly. The first phase, between the second and third century, was peaceful and gradual infiltration into the territories of the empire by individuals and groups attracted by the high standard of living of Rome and its culture. There followed a further peaceful phase of immigration and stable settlement within the Roman *limes*, not of individuals or fragmented groups but of entire peoples, destined to become states within a state. These peoples did not present themselves as regular armies, but rather as conglomerates of nomadic tribes, which included not only warriors but also women and children, animals and domestic goods.

The empire was peacefully occupied, until its borders were crossed by armed peoples who were determined to seize the wealth and power of the lands of Europe. The migrations became invasions, then occupations, and finally conquests of the Roman Empire which crumbled and finally disappeared under the weight of the barbarian surge.

In the history of the relations between the barbarians and the Roman Empire, there is a watershed date: 9 August 378. On that day, on the plain of Adrianople in Thrace, the army of the Eastern Roman Empire, led by Emperor Valens (368–378), was defeated by the Visigoths. The Roman legions were annihilated and Valens himself was killed along with many other officers. The Roman army had never known a defeat of this magnitude.

The religion of the barbarian peoples was Arianism. Valens, who was an Arian, had sent a missionary, Ulfilas, who had indoctrinated them with the Arian heresy. From then on until the sixth and seventh centuries, Arianism became the national religion of almost all the barbarian peoples installed in the territory of the empire. In addition to the Visigoths, there were the Vandals, Ostrogoths, Burgundians, Suebians, Alans, and Lombards. Some of these peoples, like the Vandals and Ostrogoths, remained Arian until their extinction in the sixth century. Others completed their religious itinerary with a second conversion to Catholicism, as was the case with the Burgundians and Visigoths in the sixth century.

Still other peoples, like the Lombards, remained Arian even beyond the seventh century. In this historical context, one can understand the importance of the conversion of the Franks on the eve of the year 500 with the baptism of King Clovis. The Franks were the only barbarian people who did not first embrace Arianism. If Valens had not made the Goths Arian, they would have become Catholic and would have spread the true Christian civilisation along with Catholicism in the barbarian world.

In this situation of chaos and decay, while the barbarians pressed at the gates, Christendom laid its definitive foundations.

The Roman State no longer had an authentic aristocracy that was aware of its role and its duties. They were no more than courtiers, nobles by title and pomp. The bishops became the most authoritative persons in their cities. Within their dioceses they had a vast, almost absolute power, that the gifts of the Holy Ghost surrounded with supernatural strength. The bishop was the administrator, judge, and the only dispenser of social welfare: everything that interested the people of God passed through his hands. It can therefore be seen that throughout the entire fourth century a true transfer of secular power into the hands of the religious authorities was underway. The Christians, writes Daniel-Rops, feeling much more supported and organised by the bishops than by government officials, thought of themselves more as children of the Church than as citizens of the empire.

The true aristocracy was found in the ranks of the Christians, an aristocracy that was simultaneously political as well as ecclesiastical. The prime example is that of Saint Ambrose, one of the first Doctors of the Western Church, of whom Theodosius would say: "Alone among all those I have known, Ambrose truly merits to be called a bishop."

2. Saint Ambrose and Theodosius

Saint Ambrose (339–397), born in Trier of a family of ancient senatorial nobility, studied in Rome and soon reached the height of his administrative career, becoming *consularis* (governor) of northern Italy with his seat in Milan, which in 364 became the capital of the Western Empire. In 374, fierce conflicts arose between the Arians and Catholics over the succession of the Arian bishop Auxentius. Ambrose, a politician who was 35 years old, was designated by both factions as bishop of Milan, despite the fact that he was only a catechumen. He received baptism and holy orders, transferred all his political and administrative functions to his new office, and proved to be an extraordinary shepherd of souls.

There are events in the life of the Church that remain etched as symbols down the course of the centuries. One of these is the showdown between Ambrose and Emperor Theodosius over the massacre of Thessalonica.

In August of 390 a revolt broke out in Thessalonica. The commander of the Roman praesidium was a Goth named Buterich. He had a homosexual arrested who was a very popular charioteer. The crowd rebelled and lynched Buterich. Theodosius was indignant, and left the Goths free to take revenge. They seized the opportunity to put on a show in the circus massacring seven thousand people by the sword. Theodosius, who had encouraged the massacre, was excommunicated by Saint Ambrose. In a private letter, full of paternal affection, the bishop implored the emperor to acknowledge his guilt, assuring him that, if he came to ask for forgiveness, he would be absolved and readmitted to Communion.

For one month, Theodosius, supported by his courtiers, balked at Ambrose's invitation. But the scruples of his conscience won. And so, on Christmas Eve in the year 390, the most powerful emperor on earth could be seen taking off his sumptuous robes and donning the humble garments of a public penitent to express his repentance in the main square of Milan before entering the Basilica of Saint Thecla, where Saint Ambrose readmitted him to the Church of Christ.

Professor Plinio Corrêa de Oliveira comments:

> "This attitude of spiritual power towards temporal power recalls a principle that is very dear to us. Regardless of his nature or title, and however exalted or glorified he may be in civil society, whenever a great person places himself in a position to challenge the glory of God, it is up to the Church to humble him.

"When human powers lose their way, it is the mission of the Church to confront them and place them in line. It is the mission of the Church to emphasise how all human affairs, no matter how elevated, are nothing before God. In the face of eternity, all human greatness is reduced to nothing. In the end, the only thing that remains forever, as a value that is above everything else, is the Holy Catholic Church, apostolic and Roman, that is, the Church of God. Bossuet affirmed this with magnificent words: 'The mission of the Church is the containment of the powers of the earth.'"

It was December 390. Ten years before, on 28 February 380, Theodosius had promulgated, in the same city of Thessalonica, an edict in which he said: "All of our people must unite in the faith transmitted to the Romans by the Apostle Peter, the faith which Pope Damasus and Bishop Peter of Alexandria profess; that is, recognising the Holy Trinity of the Father, Son and Holy Ghost."

The spiritual unity that Constantine had dared not impose, and that Julian had believed must be based on neo-paganism, was established by Theodosius by means of the principle that the empire was one, and so the faith should also be one: the orthodox Catholic faith.

Thanks to Theodosius, Arianism was definitively eradicated. In Constantinople, where Arianism was still powerful, its last protagonists were forced to give way to the Catholics, and the emperor himself enthroned the new Catholic bishop of the capital, Gregory Nazianzus, in the Church of the Holy Apostles.

In January 381, an imperial edict proclaimed the Nicene faith as a law of the State, affirming "the indivisibility of the divine substance of the Trinity" and allocating Arian goods to the "Nicenes". Finally, in the spring of that same year, the Council of Constantinople put an end to all the dogmatic questions that arose after Nicea following the spread of error. It anathematised all the "Eunomian or Anomian, Arian or Eudoxian, Semi-Arian or Pneumatomachian, Sabellian and Apollinarian" heretics, formulating a doctrine that is expressed in the Niceno-Constantinopolitan Creed, the Creed that is recited at Mass today.

3. Paganism and Christianity

The barbarians were an external enemy of the Roman Empire. But there was a more insidious enemy within the empire: resurgent paganism. The paganism of the fourth century was not the ancient religion of the Romans, but a new religious philosophy characterised by a profound relativism. This religious and cultural relativism formed a grave threat not only to Christianity but to the empire itself.

The term "paganism" comes from the Latin word *pagus*, village. The *paganalia* were the festivals of the *pagi*, the rural districts of ancient Rome (*paganicae feriae*); *paganus* meant someone who lived in the countryside, an inhabitant of the *pagus*. The etymology helps us understand how in the Roman Empire two forms of paganism co-existed. On the one hand, there were the often-superstitious beliefs of the country people, a popular paganism, which often boiled down to animistic beliefs that survived for centuries. On the other hand, among the educated classes the paganism of the fourth century was a civil religion without dogmas or morals: it was a religiosity more than a religion. It did not acknowledge any sacred texts; it did not involve any dogmas or articles of faith; it was simply a series of ritual gestures. It was a political religion, which distinguished between the public sphere, in which the polytheistic cult of the Roman gods was to be professed, and the private sphere, in which each person was free to believe in whatever he wished. It was, in the final analysis, the cult of the goddess *Roma*.

In the ancient world, alongside Roman paganism, there were also other types of paganism: Greek, Egyptian, Nordic, Celtic, Slavic. What all these forms of paganism held in common was

IV PAGAN ROME AND CHRISTIAN ROME

polytheism, that is, the veneration of a multiplicity of divinities in a true Pantheon. The word *Pantheon* (from the Greek *pan*, meaning "all", and *theos*, meaning "gods" — thus "all the gods") refers not so much to a building as to the collective whole of the divinities of a religion.

The fourth-century clash between Christianity and paganism was the clash between pagan relativism and those who, like the Christians, believed in absolute truth: Jesus Christ, the only Way, Truth, and Life (Jn 14:6). A decisive phase of the encounter between Christianity and paganism was the controversy over the Altar of Victory between Saint Ambrose and Symmachus, the two greatest representatives of two conflicting cultures.

Quintus Aurelius Symmachus (345–405) was prefect of Rome in 384 and consul in 391. Ambrose, a former imperial official, was bishop of Milan from 374 to 397. Both of them were members of ancient senatorial families; the two shared the same cultural formation, familial and social ties, but one represented the paganism that was dying, while the other represented the new Christian faith that conquered society.

In the Western Empire the pagan opposition was concentrated on the senatorial aristocracy, which continued to profess an enthusiastic veneration for Roman antiquity as well as the divinities and mysteries of the East. The centre of pagan resistance had always been the Senate. At the entrance of the Senate Chamber (*Curia Julia*), stood the Altar of Victory, placed there by Augustus on the day of his return from Egypt (28 August 29 BC). It was the public symbol of paganism. On entering the Senate Chamber, the senators performed an act of worship at the Altar of Victory, burning a grain of incense.

The Western Emperor Gratian (375–383) had ordered the removal of this altar. The Senate protested, and in 382 it sent the pagan Symmachus to Milan to obtain the revocation of this order, but Gratian, influenced by Saint Ambrose on the orders of Pope Saint Damasus (366–384), refused to receive Symmachus.

In 383 Gratian was assassinated, and Symmachus renewed his effort with Valentinian II (383–392), who succeeded his brother as emperor. Symmachus was received, and he pleaded the cause of pagan Rome, but Valentinian, persuaded by Saint Ambrose, denied permission to return the Altar of Victory (in 384). On this occasion, Symmachus, who had in the meantime become prefect of Rome, wrote his famous *Relation on the Altar of Victory*, to which Saint Ambrose responded with two letters (Letters 17 and 18) addressed to the emperor in which he warned him, under pain of excommunication, against restoring pagan cults and privileges.

The apologia Symmachus addressed to Valentinian II in the late summer of 384 was focused on religious relativism. Its motto was: "Each person has his own customs, his own religion" (*Relatio*, III, 8). It argued that there is one true God present in the diversity of religions, since "such a great mystery cannot be attained by one way alone" (*Relatio*, III, 10). Symmachus was a relativist, convinced of the unicity of a god who reveals himself in the plurality of religions. As a good pagan, Symmachus believed only in the "goddess Rome", in whose mouth he placed these words: "Princes and fathers of the homeland, respect the old age which I have reached with these sacred rites. Leave me my traditional ceremonies; I have no complaints about them. Let me live in my own way, so that I am free." When Ambrose replied, he also had Rome speak: "At this age, I do not blush to convert, along with the whole world. It is indeed true that it is never too late to learn. Let that old age blush that does not know how to correct itself" (*Epistola* 18, 7).

Ambrose then reproached Symmachus for his inconsistency: "Only now is there talk of justice and equality? Where were these speeches when Christians were not even allowed to breathe?" Ambrose claims the absolute truth of the Christian religion against all relativism. The one true God is the God of the Christians (*Ipse enim solus verus est Deus*), and there is no possibility of agreement between the two religions.

The clash between paganism and Christianity moved from the cultural to the military level and had a decisive moment in 394 in the Battle of the Frigidus, in which Theodosius defeated the last desperate effort of paganism to impose itself by force within the empire. It was a battle that, as the Roman historian Marta Sordi observes, both Christians and pagans sensed was a true war of religion.

On 15 May 392, Emperor Valentinian II was killed by his general, Arbogast, a pagan of Frankish origin. Three months later, Arbogast had the rhetorician Flavius Eugenius raised to the imperial throne. Flavius Eugenius was an apostate Christian, like Julian, and had the support of the Roman Senate. While Theodosius prohibited pagan worship in all its forms, Flavius Eugenius had the pagan Altar of Victory placed in the Senate once again and reinstituted processions through the streets of Rome in honour of the pagan divinities. Theodosius, who had not recognised Flavius Eugenius, moved towards Italy with his army in order to confront the usurper.

Saint Augustine recalls the statues of Jupiter that the pagans had put up in the Alpine passes on that occasion, while banners which bore the figure of Hercules were brought before the army (*De Civitate Dei*, V, 26). The decisive battle took place near the River Frigidus (today the Vipava, in western Slovenia), a tributary of the Isonzo, near Aquileia, between 5 and 6 September 394. The battle was marked by two extraordinary natural phenomena: in the first phase of the battle a solar eclipse gave Arbogast and Eugenius success. In the second phase, at dawn the next day, after having prayed the whole night, Theodosius was helped by a strong wind that put Arbogast's army in difficulty and Theodosius defeated his enemies.

Theodosius was only 50 years old, but in the autumn of 394, shortly after his victory over the usurpers, his health, which had never been very strong, rapidly declined. He then took measures for his succession: his firstborn son Arcadius was to rule the East, and his second son Honorius would rule the West. Theodosius intended the empire to be one, with two separate seats of authority: Constantinople and Milan. But in reality, from that year 395, the two parts of the empire, East and West, would never again be reunited.

Before he died, Theodosius received Saint Ambrose and had a long conversation with him, in which he commended his two sons to his care, asking the bishop to be their counsellor and to keep watch over the empire. Theodosius died in Milan on 17 January 395, as he piously whispered the first word of the psalm of the dead: *"Dilexi"* (Ps 116).

To his two sons — Arcadius (395–408), who was eighteen, and Honorius (395–423), who was eleven — Theodosius left an exhortation in his will to share all his devotion to the Church and his zeal for the Christian religion. Theodoret recounts his words as follows: "This religion and nothing else maintains peace and quiet in the State, bans wars, and gives the republic the strength to tame its enemies."

A few months later, while the empire was creaking and the barbarians were preparing their terrible invasion, Saint Ambrose in his turn descended to the grave, seized by forebodings and with a heart full of sadness. It was 4 April 397, the vigil of the day of the Resurrection.

4. Saint Augustine

Saint Ambrose was one of the first and greatest of the Fathers and Doctors of the Church. After his death, two other great Fathers and

IV PAGAN ROME AND CHRISTIAN ROME

Doctors of the Church kept watch as darkness fell on the Roman Empire and the light of a new world dawned: Augustine and Jerome.

Augustine was born on 13 November 354 in Thagaste, a large village in Numidia (today Souk Ahras in Algeria). Although he was born in Africa and was probably African by descent, Augustine was Roman in culture and language. His father was called Patricius. His mother Monica is venerated as a saint of the Catholic Church.

Monica, a fervent Christian, did what she could to cultivate the boy's religious sentiment; however — as was the common practice in the fourth century — she did not immediately baptise him, so that he could enjoy the full benefits of a general washing of his soul at a later time. Augustine joined the Manichaean sect, remaining there for nine years as a simple auditor (listener); in the meantime he became a professor in his native land and lived with an unnamed woman to whom he alludes frequently in his *Confessions*. For a time, astrology seduced him, but he was soon disillusioned.

Around autumn of 383, when he was 29 years old, he departed for Rome. With the support of the pagan Symmachus, he obtained a teaching chair in Milan, and there he came across some books by the neoplatonists, probably Plotinus and Porphyry. His mother, who had followed him to Milan and was a disciple of Saint Ambrose, wept and prayed for his conversion. When she asked Saint Ambrose if her son would ever be converted, the bishop answered her with the famous words: "Woman, the son of so many tears could never perish." He meant that she would see the rebirth of Augustine thanks to her intense and profound sufferings.

One can imagine her joy when Augustine received baptism from the hands of Saint Ambrose on 24 April 387. Augustine and his mother then prepared to return to Africa. Before embarking they stopped in an inn in Ostia, the port city of Rome. Standing at the window and looking at the sea, they began to speak about the things of God during the famous evening that Augustine himself recalls with emotion in his *Confessions*.

Monica died in Ostia and a few months later Augustine returned to Carthage; making, in the opposite direction, the journey which four years earlier he had made with a heart full of so many passions and uncertainties.

His elevation to the priesthood in 391 occurred in the most unforeseen way. When Valerius, the elderly bishop of Hippo, expressed his wish to be helped in public speaking by a coadjutor priest, the people acclaimed Augustine; then, in 395, Valerius himself conferred episcopal ordination on Augustine, who immediately succeeded him as bishop of Hippo. He remained bishop until his death on 28 August 430, during the third month of the siege of the city by Genseric, the king of the Vandals.

When he was made bishop of Hippo, Augustine wrote his masterpiece, the *City of God*. The theme of this extraordinary work is the perpetual and irreconcilable battle that unfolds in history between two loves that have founded two cities: "The love of self to the point of contempt for God has generated the earthly city; the love of God to the point of despising self has generated the heavenly city" (*De Civitate Dei*, book XIV, ch. 28).

The *City of God* identifies itself with the Church — triumphant, purgative, and militant — that unites the "children of light", those who are faithful to God in heaven and on earth. The Church Militant also lives in the world, but it is not of the world. It is without sin, but not without sinners.

The "earthly city" identifies itself with the *civitas diaboli*, the city of evil, understood above all as the infernal society of the damned, and as the earthly society that unites the "children of darkness" who are opposed to God. This city lives in the world, but it is not identified with the human society that lives in history.

In the midst of these two cities — the heavenly one and the infernal one — stands the "city of men", humanity that lives on the earth, a pilgrim in space and time, passing through its own period of trial. Humanity is the object of contention between the two enemy

IV PAGAN ROME AND CHRISTIAN ROME

cities, and it forms the battlefield between them. Throughout its earthly existence, humanity experiences at times the influence of the heavenly city, and at other times the influence of the infernal city. The destiny of the city of men is to tend toward either the heavenly city or the infernal one, to be governed by one or the other. *Tertium non datur* ("a third is not given"): it is not possible for humanity to remain indifferent or neutral. "If society is not consecrated to God, it is invaded by demons," says Saint Augustine. The mission of the human city is precisely that of imitating the divine city and fighting against the diabolical one.

There is a very beautiful point to consider when meditating on Saint Augustine. Plinio Corrêa de Oliveira observes that he wrote his books while the Roman Empire in the West was falling, when everything led one to think that the Catholic religion would probably be wiped out by the barbarian invasions. In fact Hippo and Carthage were so devastated that almost nothing remained standing of these cities and the Catholic religion never re-established itself in these regions with the splendour it had gained in the past. And yet while the future was uncertain, Saint Augustine continued serenely writing his books. He died as the Vandals were entering his city.

The sack of Rome by Alaric in 410 was one of the most dramatic events of antiquity. And yet, in the face of the devastation of what for them was the "goddess Rome", the great pagan rhetoricians, the disciples of Symmachus and Macrobius, fell silent. It was Saint Augustine who raised his voice before this terrible spectacle. *De Civitate Dei*, written by Saint Augustine between 413 and 426, represents the model of the Christian conception of history. The world as the saint had known it collapsed, and the Middle Ages came. The writings of Saint Augustine would inspire the medieval conception of the State, of the empire and of Christendom. Charlemagne (742–814) used to have Saint Augustine read to him while he dined and the empire he founded was inspired by the ideas of Saint Augustine.

5. Saint Jerome

Saint Jerome (347–420) is counted among the four greatest Doctors of the Western Church, along with Saint Ambrose, Saint Augustine, and Saint Gregory. Born in Stridon, in Dalmatia, in 347, he studied in Rome and was baptised there. He then went to the East, staying mostly in Antioch. Returning to Rome in 382, he became the secretary of Pope Damasus I and directed various Roman nobles to the ascetic ideal, including the matrons Marcella and Paula. He then retired to the East, and in Bethlehem he dedicated himself to what would be his life's work, the translation of the Bible from Greek and Hebrew into Latin. Saint Jerome's translation, the Vulgate, is still the official biblical text to which the Church refers today.

In his letters Saint Jerome gives a witness to the terrible events that opened the fifth century. One can say that it all began on a winter night in the year 406. On 31 December of that year, the few Roman garrisons stationed on the Rhine near Mainz spotted a swarming mass of barbarians so large that it stretched further than the eye could see beyond the river. The Rhine was a thick sheet of ice that allowed the barbarians to cross it, breaking through the borders of the empire. The few who tried to oppose them were massacred. They were Vandals, Alans, and Suebians, entire tribes, with women and children, carts, animals and flocks, who overwhelmed all resistance and spread into Gaul. Nothing could stop them. No city was spared, beginning with Trier, the ancient capital of the Western Empire. It was the beginning of the catastrophe. The two most fearsome barbarian peoples were the Vandals and the Goths, the latter being further divided into Ostrogoths and Visigoths. Other peoples, including the terrible Huns, pressed behind them.

A letter that Saint Jerome wrote from Bethlehem in 409 offers us a striking image of the situation in which the empire found itself:

"If up to this moment some of us, however few, are still at home, it is not due to our merit, but to the mercy of God. Very ferocious peoples, countless in number, have occupied all the regions of Gaul. The Quads, the Vandals, the Samaritans, the Alans, the Gepids, the Heruli, the Saxons, the Burgundians, the Alemani, and — oh, unfortunate nation! — the Pannonians, our enemies, have plundered everything between the Alps and Pyrenees, between the Ocean and the Rhine. 'Assur, in fact, fell with them.' Mainz, that once illustrious city, was taken and razed to the ground; a massacre of thousands and thousands of people was carried out in its church. The powerful city of Reims, Amiens, Arras, 'the Morini, men of the remotest edge of the world' (Virgil, *Aeneid*, VIII, 727), Tournai, the Nemesi, Strasbourg, have all had their inhabitants deported into Germany. The provinces of Aquitaine, Novempopulonia, Lyons, and Narbonne have been completely razed to the ground, except for a few small cities which however are failing due to war without and famine within. I cannot remember Toulouse without a shower of tears. If it has not been demolished thus far it is thanks to the merits of its holy bishop Exuperius.

"Even the regions of Spain are about to receive their *coup de grâce*; they live under terror each day due to the vivid memory of the invasion of the Cimbri, and they continually suffer all of the pains that others suffer once and for all due to the anticipated fear they feel about it. I will pass over everything else in silence so as not to give the impression that I may despair of God's mercy. For some time the regions contained between the Hospitable Sea [the Black Sea] and the Julian Alps and which once belonged to us have no longer been ours; and it has now been thirty years since the border of the Danube was violated and there has been fighting inside the full territory of the Roman Empire" (*Letter* 123, 15-16).

The worst was yet to come. Saint Jerome and his disciples were in Bethlehem in August 410 when an immense army of Visigoths, Huns, Alans, and Scythians, led by Alaric, reached the gates of Rome without encountering any resistance. Alaric decided to assail Rome from the north-east side of the walls, and to this end he placed his headquarters above the Salarian Bridge over the Aniene, on the hill which today is Mount Antenne. Blessed Frédérick Ozanam paints a picture of those days:

> "From the temple of Jupiter on the Capitoline one sees the smoke of the enemy camp. At this juncture, the Senate gathers and deliberates, and for its first act it has Serena the widow of Stilicho, nephew of Theodosius, killed. The gods demanded such a victim, since it was said that Christian sacrilege, which entered the temple of the Sibyl one day, had taken the collar off the idol. Serena was strangled according to ancient custom, *more maiorum*; but this last human sacrifice did not save the homeland."

On 24 August 410, the Salarian Gate was opened from within: the barbarian wave invaded Rome, and the most celebrated city in the world was mercilessly exposed to the fury of the barbarians, who lit their fires on the slopes of the Capitoline Hill. Alaric ordered them to respect the basilicas of the apostles, but gave them license to plunder everything else. Robberies, fires, and massacres desolated a city that for eight hundred years had never been invaded by an enemy.

IV PAGAN ROME AND CHRISTIAN ROME

News of the sack of Rome produced a sense of astonishment and profound consternation throughout the entire world. The sovereign city, the Eternal City, Rome, had been exposed to the outrage, ridicule, and violence of the barbarians that it had defeated a thousand times.

The pain with which Saint Jerome burst out at the successive and increasingly tragic news of the fall of the Eternal City is moving. "I was about to translate Ezekiel," he relates, "when news reached me in Palestine of the taking of Rome by Alaric and the barbaric devastation of the West; I was stupefied, and I did nothing further but weep." "The most resplendent light," he exclaimed, "has gone out; the head of the world is cut off, and in the ruin of one single city the entire empire has perished." "The city," he continued, "who subjugated all the peoples has been conquered; she who had collected and accumulated all the treasures of the earth is now despoiled and reduced to a heap of ruins."

Yet while the star of Rome was extinguished, a new light was lit: Christian Rome, the Rome of the Apostles Peter and Paul, the Rome which unlike the pagan one would defy the centuries and millennia. The light of this Rome which never sets continues to illuminate the world, even when the world seems to be immersed in darkness as it is today. The modern world seems to be following the self-destructive path of the Roman Empire. The Church of Rome is destined to rise over the ruins of the modern world, as already happened once before in the fifth century.

Radio Maria, 21 December 2011

CHAPTER V

Why the Roman Empire fell

1. The decline of the Roman Empire

The comparison made by Pope Benedict XVI between the crisis of our time and the crisis at the time of the decline of the Roman Empire provides the starting point for a reflection that deserves to be expanded.

The word "decline" refers to a historical period which cannot be confined to just a few short years. We know that the official date of the fall of the Roman Empire in the West is AD 476. In that year, the barbarian Odoacer, after killing his rival Orestes, deposed the last emperor, the young Romulus Augustus, and sent the imperial insignia back to Byzantium, contenting himself with the title of king. From that time on, the emperor of the East claimed the legacy of Rome, at least until the year AD 800, when Charlemagne was crowned as emperor and the ancient Roman Empire was resurrected in the West as the Holy Roman Empire.

But the institutional crisis of the Roman Empire, which came about in 476 with the disappearance of the visible empire in the West, went back at least a century. We have already recalled the year 378, when the Roman legions were defeated by the Visigoths on the plain of Adrianople and Valens II, the emperor of the West, fell on the battlefield. It was the most serious defeat for the Roman army since the Battle of Cannae in 216 BC. The Battle of Adrianople marks the first great military victory of the barbarians over Rome, and it opened the way for the great invasions which characterised the fifth century, the century of the definitive decline of the Roman Empire.

V WHY THE ROMAN EMPIRE FELL

The external cause of the decline and then the collapse of the Roman Empire was the barbarian invasions. But the true and deeper causes of the decadence and end of the Roman Empire were internal and of a cultural and moral nature. While the barbarian peoples threatened the borders of an immense empire that stretched from the Atlantic Ocean and the North Sea all the way to North Africa, the Caspian Sea, and the borders with the Persians and Arabs, Roman society was immersed, as a result of paganism, in an intellectual relativism and a practical hedonism. Thus Benedict XVI affirmed in relation to the Roman Empire that the "breakdown of the fundamental systems of law and of the moral attitudes that gave them strength, caused the cracks to appear in the dams that up until that time had protected peaceful coexistence among men. A world was declining." It was moral corruption that opened the gates to the Vandals, who crossed the frozen Rhine and broke into Gaul in 406, and to the Visigoths, who invaded Rome in 410.

In order to understand the significance of these events, we must refer first of all to the authors of the time like Orosius, Augustine, Jerome, and Salvian. Saint Jerome, for example, in a famous letter, writing from the solitude of Bethlehem where he had retired, relates the news that had come to him from Rome following the arrival of Alaric's Visigoths outside the city walls:

> "From the West comes to us the terrible news that Rome is being besieged, that the safety of its citizens is being bought for their weight in gold, but that after these extortions the siege is resumed: those who have already been deprived of their possessions are also being deprived of their lives. My voice fails, weeping prevents me from dictating. The city that conquered the whole world has been conquered: indeed, it falls from hunger even before it falls by force of arms, so much so that there is hardly anyone to take prisoner. Desperate greed makes people throw themselves

on vile foods: the famished people tear each other apart; even the mother does not spare her nursing child and swallows into her stomach that which she has just given birth to."

These are chilling scenes that allow us to understand the extent of the tragedy. When refugees from Rome later began to seek refuge in the East and also in Bethlehem, they described the gruesome scenes of the sack of the city. Jerome wept for sorrow and wrote: "Who would have believed that Rome, built with victories all over the world, would one day collapse? Or that all the shores of the East, of Egypt, and of Africa would be populated with slaves, men and women fleeing from the city that was once the ruler of the world? Or that the holy city of Bethlehem would welcome people of both sexes now reduced to begging, who shortly before were nobles laden with riches?" He further exclaimed, "The brightest light has gone out, the Roman Empire's head has been cut off, and by the ruin of one single city the entire empire has been extinguished."

These words make us reflect on how precarious and ephemeral is every human honour, power, and wealth. It was precisely in meditating on the sack of Rome in 410 that Saint Augustine composed his famous *City of God*, one of the greatest Christian philosophical works concerning the history of humanity, conceived as the history of the battle between two loves: the love of self to the point of hatred of and indifference towards God and the love of God to the point of hatred of and indifference towards oneself. This vision of history has not lost its relevance.

The Roman Empire collapsed because within it the moral and divine law had been transgressed. This is what history attests, and so the study of history speaks to us as a warning. Once again today, foreign peoples are invading the West. It is a peaceful and silent migration that could, however, turn into a bloody invasion. The barbarians were foreign to Roman civilisation but assimilated its culture and traditions. The new barbarians proclaim that they do

V WHY THE ROMAN EMPIRE FELL

not want to integrate into our civilisation, of which they assimilate only the elements of decadence, rejecting its culture and traditions.

Even today the heart of man — and as a result the life of society — oscillates between two opposing callings. On the one hand, there is the love of God, which is expressed by a respect for the order that He has given to the universe, to the point of renouncing our instincts and desires, so as to preserve this order. On the other hand, there is the love of ourselves, leaving free rein to our passions and our will to have power, to the point of transgressing the law of God in our own lives and in society. These are the dramatic alternatives that always arise in history, in the face of which not only individual people but also entire civilisations are called to make a choice.

In the darkness of the fifth century, only the light of the saints shone forth. They were the ones who understood what was happening and instilled supernatural confidence when all seemed lost. "Christ is speaking to you; listen!" exclaimed Saint Augustine. "He says to you, 'Why are you afraid?' Didn't I predict all this to you? I predicted it so that when the sentence arrived your hope would turn towards the true good, instead of growing dim in the world." Everything that happens in history, just as in the life of each one of us, has a meaning and a significance known only by God.

"Do you complain," wrote another prophetic voice, the priest Salvian of Marseilles, "that God is allowing everything to fall into ruin? But no, God governs the world! It is not true that he does not take care of the earth: it is indeed the object of all his care!" If many disasters occur, the cause must be sought in ourselves. "It is our sins that make the barbarians strong," exclaimed Saint Jerome, "it is our vices that have weakened the armies!"

The saints illuminated the darkest hours in history without seeing the results of their faith in the ages that followed.

Twenty years after the sack of Rome by Alaric's Visigoths, Genseric's Vandals came from Gaul, passing through Spain and across

Gibraltar, spreading into Africa and occupying all of the territory from Morocco to Carthage.

The horrors committed by the Vandals in Africa are narrated by Saint Augustine: children sliced in two, virgins tortured with burning irons applied to their breasts, and many important people impaled.

In the year 430, in the citadel of Hippo besieged by the Vandals, the bishop who for 34 years had guided the faithful of that city saw that the end was near, and with it the end of all of Christian Africa. And yet in the face of this total collapse, Augustine galvanised souls and instilled in the resisters a supernatural confidence that went far beyond the earthly destiny of those regions. His voice rose over the centuries and repeated the divine word: "Heaven and earth shall pass, but my words shall not pass" (Mt 24:35). It was only when his voice fell silent that the Vandals stormed the city.

During those same years, Saint Nicasius allowed himself to be killed in the cathedral of Reims, slowing down the Vandals so that more of his people could escape. Saint Exuperius, the bishop of Toulouse, resisted the Vandals until his deportation. Saint Lupus defended Troyes, where he was bishop. Saint Eucherius of Lyons defended the rights of the Church against the Burgundians. Saint Anianus, bishop of Orléans, organised the defence of his city against the Huns and encouraged the people to resist, permitting the Roman legions of Egypt to reach Attila and defeat him. Saint Paulinus became the bishop of Nola just when Alaric was at the city gates and offered himself as a slave to the invaders in order to ransom the only son of a widow. Quodvultdeus, the holy bishop of Carthage and former deacon of Saint Augustine, organised the resistance against the occupying Vandals until he was chased from his see by Genseric and placed on a boat without sails or oars, which miraculously arrived in Naples, where he died as a confessor of the faith. Saint Maximus, the first bishop of Turin, and Saint Peter Chrysologus, the bishop of Ravenna, were simultaneously hammers of heretics and indefatigable defenders of the threatened civilisation.

Once again today, it is necessary to draw strength from the Christian virtues against the physical evil that threatens us from the outside and the moral evil that strikes us from within.

It is strikingly reminiscent of the last days of Rome that today's accusations against our political class of living a morally decadent life, are made by those who have made moral relativism their programme.

In Italy and in Europe there is a moral crisis, but only those who make reference to perennial and non-negotiable values have the right to intervene in this matter. How can those who deny these values in principle reprove others who transgress them? These are the contradictions of the current era, but contradiction is the distinguishing characteristic of relativism.

2. A greying world

Between the fourth and fifth centuries after Christ, the barbarians who invaded the northern and eastern provinces of the empire, conquering them and devastating their cities, reached the extreme confines of the Atlantic and Mediterranean, sacking Rome, the *caput mundi*, the sacred and inviolate city which had dictated laws to the entire civilised world.

This enemy that Rome had to face and by which it would ultimately be overwhelmed was an external enemy. But the deepest cause of the collapse of the Roman Empire was actually not something external but internal. It was not political or military in nature but had a cultural and moral cause. The Roman Empire collapsed because the edifice was now rotten and its strength was nothing more than an empty show. Let us seek to develop this point too in order to better understand the crisis of our own time.

The decline of the Roman Empire, considered under the aspect of external causes — the barbarian invasions — took place between 378, when the barbarians overwhelmed the Roman legions at Adrianople, and 476, the year of the official disappearance of the Western Empire. The cultural and moral crisis, however, does not go back merely to the fourth or fifth century: it preceded this and may be attributed to the lack of understanding and hostility that the Roman Empire showed towards Christianity.

In the centuries that followed the birth of Christ, the Roman Empire professed an ecumenical religiosity that blended Greco-Roman polytheism with a syncretism of eastern origin. The place *par excellence* of this civil religion was the Pantheon, which welcomed all forms of paganism, both new and old, and excluded only one religion: Christianity.

In the empire, a civil religion was professed, without either dogmas or morals, towards which the State required a purely formal adherence. The Christians, who practised a religion that was first of all interior, a religion of the heart and of the conscience that submitted to an objective truth, refused this formal adherence, which was expressed by burning incense to idols.

The witness of Christians was considered a form of dangerous intransigence and fanaticism by those authorities who also professed the syncretistic equivalence of all religions. The sentence that condemned Christians did not make specific charges but rather targeted the *nomen ipsum*, the simple proclamation of one's Christianity.

The persecutions reached their peak with Emperor Diocletian, who reigned until the year 305. It was one of the darkest periods in the history of the Church. And yet, just a few years later, a new emperor, Constantine, granted full liberty to Christians. Finally they could profess their faith publicly and infuse their spirit into the laws promulgated in those years. It was the great Constantinian shift. The ascent of Christianity, from Constantine to Theodosius, was irresistible. But paganism did not give up, and

V WHY THE ROMAN EMPIRE FELL

in the fourth century it waged a deadly battle against the name "Christian".

The brief reign of Emperor Julian the Apostate, between 361 and 363, was the most acute expression of pagan hatred for Christians, who were forbidden from holding magistracies and teaching positions or being awarded honours and dignities. After the death of Julian, the centre of anti-Christian sentiment was the Roman Senate, the Senate that in AD 37, just a few years after the death of Jesus Christ, had vetoed Christianity with a *senatus consultus.*

Paganism in the second half of the fourth century was no longer a religion but a relativistic philosophy which placed all the religious cults at the same level, as opposed to Christianity which affirmed the uniqueness of Christ, the only Way, Truth, and Life. The anti-pagan policy of Emperor Theodosius at the end of the fourth century did not succeed in extirpating this relativistic mentality, which shielded the Roman Pantheon against Christianity.

For the Christians of the fourth century, paganism was an enemy worse than the barbarians, because it was an internal enemy that prevented the Roman Empire from fully embracing Christianity. The Gospel did not succeed in stopping the moral disintegration of the upper classes, who lived in luxury and idleness, nor that of the populace, who got drunk on the bloody games of the circus. Divorce, male and female prostitution, homosexuality, and a low birth rate spread everywhere. The society of this era was so decadent and corrupt that Saint Eucherius, the bishop of Lyons, called it "a greying world".

3. Salvian of Marseilles

We have recalled Saint Augustine's meditation on the fall of Rome, which the bishop of Hippo began to compose in 410 after the sack of the Visigoths. He finished his writing just as the Vandals, passing through Gibraltar, were about to conquer Roman Africa. Less well known, but equally striking and profound, is the meditation of another Christian author of the fifth century, Salvian of Marseilles, in *De Gubernatione Dei* (*On the Government of God*). It is a work that I have already mentioned, but which never loses its relevance.

Salvian, after recounting how the members of the Senate of Trier, in Germany, were intent on feasting just as the barbarians entered the city and could not bring themselves to decide to interrupt the feast, recalls that:

> "While the barbarians' weapons clattered around the walls of Cirta and Carthage, the community of Carthage gave itself over to mad joy in the circuses and became soft in the theatres. Outside the walls people were being slaughtered, while inside people fornicated. Outside, one part of the population was a prisoner of their enemies, while the other part, inside, was a prisoner of its vices. It is difficult to say who had the worst fate: the former endured a purely physical, bodily captivity, while the others were slaves interiorly. Of these two fatal misfortunes, I think that the lighter one, for a Christian, would be to undergo slavery of the body rather than that of the soul; and this is confirmed by what is said by the Saviour himself in the Gospel: the death of the soul is much more serious than the death of the body. … Both outside and inside the walls was heard a roar of battles and amusements: the screams of those who were dying mixed with the din of those who gave themselves to orgies, and one could scarcely distinguish the laments of the people who were dying in battle because of the noise produced by the people in the circus. Faced with such facts, what else did a rabble like that do other than call down its own destruction while God, probably, did not yet intend to send them to hell?"

V WHY THE ROMAN EMPIRE FELL

Carthage, the capital of Roman Africa, contended with Alexandria and Antioch for the primacy of debauchery and enjoyed the reputation of being the "paradise" of homosexuals. Salvian interpreted the invasion of the barbarians as a chastisement for this moral transgression.

"I ask you, could one give an example of a more unnatural vice than the one I am now speaking of, there in Carthage? ... In Carthage this vice was no small thing, but a plague, even if the transvestites were not actually many in number; it happened however that the effeminacy of a few infected the majority. It is known that even though only a few may take on shameless attitudes, many people will be infected with the obscenities of that minority. A single prostitute, for example, causes many men to fornicate; and the same thing happens with the abominable presence of a few homosexuals: they infect a lot of people. And I do not know who is more guilty before God, since both homosexuals and their victims are condemned to the same punishment, according to sacred scripture: 'Effeminate men and homosexuals will have no part in the kingdom of God'.

"Now, what arouses the most pain and consternation is that a crime like that was seen from the outside as belonging to the entire Roman Empire, and that all of the prestige of the name of Rome was reduced to ashes thanks to the infamous stain of that monstrous crime against nature. And the reason is this: when the males dressed as women and walked swaying worse than women do, when they tied on pendants depicting monstrous obscenities and covered their heads with feminine veils and clasps; when all this happened publicly in a Roman city, the largest and most famous of that province, was it not a disgrace for the entire Roman Empire that such an abhorrent scandal was openly permitted in the very heart of the State? In reality, if a great and powerful authority is aware of a major crime, has the power to prevent it, and yet allows it to be perpetrated, it is as if it approves its perpetration. I repeat the question, driven by distress, to those who get annoyed with me: among what barbarian peoples have such deeds ever occurred? Where under the sun have they ever been allowed to be committed with impunity?"

Salvian wants to show that the judgment of God is not carried out only at the end of the world but at every historical moment, and that the barbarians who invaded the West were an instrument of the judgment of God. Providence, which draws good from evil, used them to purify a corrupt and decadent society like Rome. The words of Salvian are worthy of meditation. Today we live in an era in which the worst vices are nourished by the mass media and are even written into laws as human rights. God, however, is not uninterested in what happens in history. He draws good from every evil, but every evil must have its punishment, in time or in eternity, just as in the same manner every good must have its reward.

4. Saint Leo the Great

Pagan hedonism was one of the principal causes of the collapse of the Roman Empire, but it was not the worst enemy that Christianity had to face. The barbarians were an enemy that were external to the empire, while hedonistic paganism was an enemy internal to the empire but external to Christianity. There was, however, an even more insidious enemy, internal to Christianity itself, and this was an enemy worse than the barbarians and paganism: the spirit of division and rebellion, of schisms and heresies that began to undermine the solid unity of Christians.

V WHY THE ROMAN EMPIRE FELL

In the year 313, with the Edict of Milan, Constantine had granted full liberty to Christians. The Church exulted. A few years later, in 325, Emperor Constantine had convoked the First Ecumenical Council in Nicea, in which the Catholic *symbolon* had been proclaimed against the Arians, and was labelled "Athanasian" by the enemies of Saint Athanasius, the bishop of Alexandria, the purest champion of the orthodox faith. But Arianism penetrated into the bishops themselves, and not ten years had passed since Nicea when two synods, at Caesarea and Tyre, condemned Saint Athanasius for his fanaticism in ecclesiastical matters. Athanasius was deposed from his cathedra and exiled. From that time on, his life summed up, so to speak, the fate of the Catholic faith. Five times he was sent into exile, and five times he returned in order to reaffirm the truth of the faith.

It came to the point that in 357, Pope Liberius broke communion with Saint Athanasius, declaring him to be separated from the Roman Church. In 359 the Council of Rimini and Seleucia proposed an equivocal *via media* between the Arians and Saint Athanasius. It was of this time that that Saint Jerome coined the expression according to which "the whole world groaned and was astonished to find itself Arian".

The middle of the fourth century was one of the most confused eras in history, in which, according to Cardinal Newman, the dogma of the divinity of Jesus Christ was preserved more by the peoples faithful to their baptism than by the *ecclesia docens*.

When Arianism was finally defeated at the end of the fourth century, new devastating heresies arose, such as Donatism and Pelagianism. Catholics once again became divided, and at the beginning of the fifth century Saint Augustine became what Saint Athanasius had been in the preceding century: a champion of the orthodox faith.

Babel reigned among the Christians who did not present a cohesive body before the double enemy that was before them: paganism within the empire and barbarians without. This situation of confusion and general disorientation constituted the deepest reason for the decline of the Roman Empire, a decline that was spiritual and moral before it was political, economic, or social.

It was not difficult for the barbarians to prevail, and the fifth century was one of the darkest hours in the history of the West. And yet in the midst of this darkness a star shone: while the Roman Empire was disintegrating, a new empire was born in Rome, not political but spiritual, which embraced the souls of the whole world, which defied the centuries; which still stands today, at the hour of this new decline — no longer the decline of the Roman Empire but the decline of the West — when new barbarians press at the gates and new pagans persecute Christians within.

Dom Guéranger writes:

> "The empire would fall piece by piece under the blows of the barbarians, but before inflicting humiliation and punishment upon it, as a consequence of its age-old crimes, divine justice would wait for Christianity, victorious over the persecutions, to have extended its branches high enough and far enough in order to dominate the waves of this new flood everywhere; it will then be seen to cultivate once more and with full success the earth renewed and reinvigorated by these purifying though devastating waters".

Night fell on the West, but a light shone in the darkness, announcing a new day of history. The authors of the fifth century see this light in the papacy, the first great European institution that rose out of the ruins of Roman civilisation. Prosper of Aquitaine, a disciple of Saint Augustine, and author of the work entitled *The Call of All Nations*, sees Pope Leo I, the man who succeeded in saving Rome from the invasion of Attila, as the protagonist of this rebirth. It was August 452 when a Roman delegation, headed by Pope Leo,

V WHY THE ROMAN EMPIRE FELL

faced Attila, the leader of the Huns, at the Mincio River. We do not know the words Leo addressed to him, but Attila, the scourge of God, turned back, abandoned Italy, and Saint Leo the Great saved Rome, triumphantly refuting the criticisms of the pagans who attributed the loss of the empire to the Christians.

Christian Rome, founded by the Apostles Peter and Paul, was now taking the place of ancient pagan Rome founded by Romulus and Remus. No other empire attained the splendour of the Roman Empire. It seemed to have been made to last for thousands of years, but it too was subject to the law of time and history. The only thing left today of pagan Rome is ruins. It is the law of everything that is human and earthly — great successes and worldly triumphs are followed, with even greater rapidity, by decadence, decay and death. Pius XII reminded us of this in his speech of 30 January 1944:

> "When we find ourselves before the testimonies of the Christian past, no matter how ancient they may be, we always feel something immortal: the faith which they proclaim still lives, multiplied indefinitely in the number of those who profess it: the Church still lives, to which they belong, always the same through the centuries."

Saint Leo the Great (440–461) was the great architect of the Romanisation of Christianity which took place in the fifth century while the Western Roman Empire was collapsing. "God," he writes, "took care that the peoples were united in a single empire, of which Rome was the head, so that from this empire the light of truth revealed for the salvation of all the nations would spread more effectively in all its members".

Leo was the great protagonist of his century — the fifth century — which saw the definitive fall of the Western Roman Empire. No one was as fully aware as he was of the inexorable decline of Rome, but also of the ascent of a new Rome, whose empire would be much vaster and more glorious than that of the ancients.

Radio Maria, 19 January 2011

CHAPTER VI
The conversion of the European nations

1. The conversion of Clovis

In the darkest epochs of history, when everything seems lost and nothing seems humanly possible, divine grace is able to produce miraculous and unexpected revivals in order to change the course things. This can still happen today. It certainly happened in the fifth century after Christ, one of the darkest periods in the history of the Church. The Roman Empire was collapsing, but from its ruins the Christian civilisation of the Middle Ages was born. This new chapter in the history of Christianity and European civilisation began with the conversion of King Clovis and his people, the Franks.

The land of the Franks was a wild and forested region in the heart of Europe, on the two banks of the Rhine. The Franks were a proud and courageous people of Germanic origin, like the Sicambri, another barbarian tribe which mixed with them. When the Franks crossed the Rhine and settled in Roman Gaul in the fourth century, they entered a territory that had already been evangelised through the work of ardent apostles like Saint Irenaeus of Lyons, Saint Denis and Saint Germain in Paris, Saint Saturninus in Toulouse, Saint Martial in Limoges, Saint Benignus in Dijon, and Saint Nicasius in Reims. During the first three centuries, the blood of the martyrs had been spilt in Gaul and in all the territories subject to the empire. But, with the advent of Constantine, Christianity had emerged from the catacombs. Then, in the fifth century, Christian Gaul had been conquered by the pagan tribe of the Franks.

Born around 466, Clovis was a warrior of Germanic origin who assumed power in 482 as the king of the Salians, a Frankish tribe. At the time of his coming, Roman Gaul had been shattered into various kingdoms: in the southwest, the kingdom of the Visigoths with its capital in Toulouse, which included the regions of Gaul south of the Loire and Spain; in the southeast, between Lyons and Geneva, the kingdom of the Burgundians, which was further divided between three brothers who were all sovereigns; and in the northeast the kingdom of the Franks, now led by Clovis.

A distant affinity linked the Franks to the kingdom of Christ. The birth of the Divine Redeemer had been preceded by extraordinary events: while the star guided the Magi from the East towards Bethlehem, Emperor Augustus, although unaware of the full significance of his action, had ordered the temple of Janus to be closed as a sign that peace in the world had been achieved under his reign. In order for this to happen, it had first been necessary to definitively defeat the tribes of the Sicambri and the Franks, who for many years had kept the Roman legions in check in the forests of Germany. So it was done. On Christmas Eve, the news of their submission arrived in Rome and it could finally be said that peace reigned in the world. The prince of peace announced by the prophets, the Saviour, was born in Bethlehem in a world that was temporarily at peace, and as Abbé Lemann writes, the Franks and the Sicambri were, so to speak, the messengers that peace had been achieved on earth during the time of Augustus.

Four centuries would pass, however, before divine grace touched the Frankish people. The instrument of grace was a young Burgundian princess named Clothilde who lived in the southern region of Gaul near Lyons. Burgundy was then divided into two kingdoms ruled by two brothers, Gundobad and Godegisel. Another brother, Chilperic, had been defeated and perhaps murdered. His widow and his two daughters, one of whom was Clothilde, were Catholic, even if in Burgundy the majority of the people and the two kings professed the Arian faith. The Burgundians, in fact, had converted from paganism to Catholicism, but around 440 they switched to Arianism under violent pressure from the Visigoths.

Clothilde, the daughter of King Childeric, was born around 475, almost exactly at the same time as the fall of the Roman Empire in the West (476). She was not yet twenty years old when an unexpected messenger came to the palace of her uncle, King Gundobad.

King Clovis had called his most trusted servant, Aurelian, and commissioned him with an engagement ring to give to Clothilde with the request of matrimony. The messenger disguised himself as a beggar, and when he arrived in Lyons he tried to meet Clothilde at the entrance of the church where the young princess gave alms to the poor of the city like an angel of charity. When Clothilde appeared, Aurelian approached her and begged her to listen to an important message that he had for her. He confided to her that he had been sent by the king of the Franks, who wanted to marry her, and he gave her the ring.

Clothilde was troubled, as Our Lady was when the archangel Gabriel appeared to her, and she responded with a soft voice, "How can this happen? It is not permitted for a Christian woman to marry a pagan prince." Aurelian assured her of Clovis' favourable dispositions towards the Church and his desire to choose a Catholic woman as his queen. Clothilde then responded: "If through this union I can bring your master to know the true God, then I accept." The young princess made the sign of the cross, accepted Clovis' ring, and gave her own ring in exchange for it, saying to the messenger: "Return quickly to your master and tell him to ask King Gundobad for permission to marry me without delay, because any delay would be a danger."

Clovis' ambassadors came to Gundobad for the official request, and when asked, Clothilde revealed that she had already received Clovis' ring and had accepted his offer of marriage. Gundobad grumbled, but he did not dare to challenge Clovis with a refusal, since the young king of the Franks was already known for his pride and valour. Aurelian took charge of the princess, taking her on a chariot pulled by oxen to be the bride of his master. Two days later, however, King Gundobad went back on his decision and sent his knights out in pursuit of Clothilde. The young princess, warned in time, abandoned the chariot, and mounting a fast steed succeeded in reaching Frankish territory. Her marriage to Clovis was celebrated in 493 at Soissons.

From then on, Clothilde had only one thought: converting the pagan king who had become her spouse. The desire in the heart of the king to make his wife happy clashed with his fear of provoking the pagan gods and displeasing the warriors he commanded, who were imbued with pagan superstitions. When she became a mother, Clothilde obtained the baptism of the young heir, but when the child died immediately after his baptism, Clovis burst into reproaches: "If we had consecrated him to the pagan gods he would still be alive!" The young mother replied with sweet firmness: "I adore my God in this trial, and I thank Him for having done me the honour of recalling my son to Himself, in order to give Him a place among the angels."

A year later, a second son was born, who was baptised with the name Chlodomer. The Lord allowed him to fall ill as well, arousing Clovis' irritation, but as Gregory of Tours recounts, "Clothilde prayed so much for the health of the child that God granted it to her." The queen did not cease to pray for the conversion of her husband, and this petition too did not remain unanswered. This all happened in the year 496. The Alemanni, one of the most ferocious Germanic tribes, had penetrated into Gaul. Clovis confronted them at Tolbiac, near Cologne. Both sides fought furiously, but the Franks, who were inferior in number, were on the point of succumbing. Clovis sought the help of his gods in vain. Turning to heaven with a thundering voice that for a moment dominated the roar of the fray, he exclaimed: "God of Clothilde, give me victory and I will give myself to you!" The name of Clothilde thus hovered over the plain of Tolbiac, and the God of Hosts accepted the naïve but fervent prayer of this barbarian. The fortunes of the battle suddenly changed. Clovis' soldiers seemed to multiply, the Alemanni began to flee, and Clovis became the master of the battlefield. Now it was up to him to keep his promise. He did not wait to meet the unsuspecting Clothilde, but on his way back he had himself instructed in the rudiments of the catechism by the holy hermit Vaast, the future bishop of Arras, who rode alongside him. When the queen came to meet him along the way, the victorious warrior addressed himself to her as follows: "Clothilde, it is not I who defeated the Germans, it was your God! And you, Clothilde, have conquered Clovis!" Clothilde responded, "To God alone be the glory for these two triumphs."

Saint Remigius (c.440–c.533), then the bishop of Reims, introduced Clovis to the mysteries of the Christian faith, and the Frankish king himself became an apostle of the faith to his comrades in arms. He was deeply moved in listening to the account of the Passion of Our Lord, and placing his hand on the hilt of his sword, he exclaimed: "Ah, if only I had been there with my Franks!" "From this impulse of chivalrous generosity," writes Abbé Lemann, "the soul of Christian France was born."

One day the bishop Remigius, as he stood in front of Clovis and Clothilde kneeling in prayer, was imploring the Blessed Virgin Mary's protection of the Christian king of the Franks, when suddenly the church was flooded by a celestial light and a supernatural perfume, and he heard a voice that said: "Peace be with you! Do not be afraid; persevere in my love." Clovis and Clothilde prostrated themselves to the ground, while the holy bishop proclaimed: "Your posterity will govern this realm nobly. It will glorify the holy Church and will inherit the empire of the Romans. It will not cease to prosper so long as it follows the ways of truth and virtue. Its decline can only come from evil habits."

Saint Remigius wanted the conversion of Clovis to be celebrated with all the pomp that the event deserved. It was Christmas Day of the year 496. The Church of Reims was illuminated by a thousand perfumed candles, and when the royal procession reached it, preceded by the cross and the sacred oil of baptism, as Gregory of Tours relates in the *History of the Franks*, the voice of Remigius was heard resounding solemnly in the basilica: "Bend your head meekly, O Sicamber; adore what you have burned; burn what you have adored."

As the officials behind Clovis, divided into groups, received baptism, the other soldiers beat their lances loudly on their shields crying out: "Christmas! Christmas!" In a letter to Clovis, the bishop of Vienne, Saint Avitus, wrote: "Choosing for yourself, you choose for all. Your faith is our victory." Blessed Frédéric Ozanam writes that when Clovis and his three thousand companions came out of the basilica regenerated and reinvigorated by baptism, there came with them fourteen centuries of monarchy, and with them, the chivalry, the Crusades, scholasticism and all the greatness of the centuries to come.

But another miracle would also mark that date. In the primitive Church the forehead of the baptised person was anointed with holy oil immediately following the actual baptism. On that day the cleric who carried the sacred chrism to the baptismal font did not succeed in arriving due to the crowd that thronged around the church. The ceremony was suspended. Then Saint Remigius turned his eyes to heaven, and weeping copiously, he began to pray in silence. And behold a dove appeared, whiter than snow, which carried a small cruet in its beak full of sacred chrism: an oil that had not been extracted from earthly plants but came directly from the heavenly gardens. Anointing the forehead of the king with this chrism, Saint Remigius impressed a supernatural seal there. The same cruet was then used in the coronation of the kings of France from Louis the Pious to Louis XVI. It was shattered by the Jacobins during the French Revolution, but the fragments were recovered and the chrism was used again, after the revolution and Napoleon, for the coronation of Charles X as king of France in 1824.

Abbé Lemann observes that all the nations of Europe, in their response to the divine call, in a certain sense fulfilled and completed the mystery of the Epiphany; the Magi being, according to the unanimous testimony of the Fathers of the Church, *primitiae Gentium* — the first fruits of the Gentiles. For France the mystery of Christmas was added to that of the Epiphany, since it was on the very day that the redeemer was born that the Franks received baptism, entering into the Church as one entire people.

As if to supernaturally confirm this vocation, three centuries later on Christmas Day, another king of the Franks, Charlemagne, would be crowned as emperor in Saint Peter's in Rome. And just as had happened three centuries earlier, the swords would beat on the shields in the Constantinian Basilica to the cry of, "Christmas! Christmas!" According to Daniel-Rops this scene of the baptism of Clovis constitutes, along with the vision of Constantine and the coronation of Charlemagne, one of the three events that determined the political destiny of the Christian West. This should not be forgotten.

Six years later Clovis marched against Alaric II, the king of the Visigoths. In 507 at Vouillé he defeated him, taking over the entire country from the Loire to the Pyrenees. He impressed a religious character on this Franco-Visigoth war, the first between the Catholic north of Gaul against the heretical south. When he had everything prepared for the enterprise, he said to his military leaders: "It is gravely painful to me that these Arians own part of Gaul. Let us go with the help of God and, after conquering them, let us submit their country to our dominion."

The dominion of the Visigoths in France was shattered. In these lands the Roman faith was now in the ascendency. Clovis thus broke the grave threat of a barbarian and Arian west. Prior to him, the Gothic world stretched from the Danube to the Rhine and the Loire and all the way to Gibraltar. At the heart of this Arian world, Clovis was the driving force of the Catholic faith.

Clovis established the capital of his new kingdom in Paris, which was then a tiny unknown city called Lutetia. He accepted with great pride the title of Roman consul which was sent to him from Byzantium by Emperor Anastasius, who thus recognised him as a representative of the Roman world. He convoked a national Council of the Church at Orléans at which 32 bishops participated, imitating what Constantine had done at Nicea.

It has been said that Clovis united three elements for the first time: the Germanic, the Roman, and the Catholic. In his person, the barbarian became civilised, the German became Romanised, and the pagan became Catholic.

Clovis died in Paris on 27 November 511 at the age of 45. He was the founder of the first royal dynasty of France, the Merovingian dynasty, and with him France became "the eldest daughter of the Church". The Frankish armies, from Clovis to Charlemagne, would be bearers of the Catholic faith.

Alongside his name we must not however forget the name of his wife, Saint Clothilde. Widowed after 20 years of marriage, the queen of the Franks suffered many trials until she retired to Tours to be near the tomb of Saint Martin, to whom she was particularly devoted. In that region she founded churches and monasteries, giving herself to penance and works of charity. She died there on 3 June 545. Afterwards her body was transported to Paris and laid alongside the bodies of Clovis and Saint Geneviève (c.422–c.502), the patron of the capital. Her mortal remains were then cremated in 1793 to avoid profanation at the time of the Revolution. They now rest in a basilica dedicated to her that was built between 1846 and 1856. Each year on 3 June Saint Clothilde is solemnly commemorated in this church. Clothilde is also responsible for the three lilies on the coat of arms of the French monarchy, after she received a shield with lilies on it as a gift from a mysterious hermit in the forest of Saint-Germain-en-Laye.

Clovis and Clothilde were great devotees of Saint Martin (c.315–397), a soldier from Roman Pannonia (today Slovakia), who was destined, as monk and bishop, to become a patron saint of the French nation, the protector of the Merovingian dynasty, and of the expansion of the kingdom of the Franks. He was one of the most important evangelisers of pagan Gaul. His disciple Sulpicius Severus wrote that "truly before Martin very few people, indeed almost none, had accepted the name of Christ in these regions. This name was imbued with such miraculous power and because of his example there is now no longer any place which is not full of numerous churches or monastic centres. Where he had destroyed temples, he immediately built churches and monasteries." The mission of Saint Martin, writes Dom Guéranger, was to truly complete the defeat of paganism, which whilst it had been expelled from the city of the martyrs, it remained the master of the vast countrysides where the influence of the city was not felt.

In 470, about ten years before Clovis became king of the Franks, a great basilica was built in Tours over the tomb of Saint Martin, which was already famous in all of Gaul because of the miracles that had taken place there. This basilica was destined, along with the church of Reims and the church of Saint Denis, to become for long centuries a spiritual centre of France; they were also tied to the Christianisation of the nation and its monarchy.

The idea of a Christian monarchy, which flourished after Theodosius in the fifth century, remained alive in Western thought thanks to Clovis. His conversion and his reign predestined the Franks for the future Christian empire.

According to Father Grisar, "Whoever in the course of the great upheavals of the fifth century wants to look for a climactic point in history which can be designated as the beginning of the Middle Ages, cannot find a better date than 496, at least in some sense, in the exaltation of Clovis and his baptism ... since these events had an impact among the Franks that was much deeper in the development of humanity than the disappearance of imperial succession ... While the Franks entered into the Church without passing through Arianism, the remaining German peoples, apart from those who still lived in the darkness of paganism, were Arian."

In the year 567, in the kingdom of the Franks, the poet Venantius Fortunatus (530–607) became the secretary of Queen Radegund in the monastery of Poitiers, where he composed a famous hymn, the *Vexilla Regis Prodeunt*. Emperor Justin II (520–576), beseeched by Radegund, sent a relic of the Holy Cross in a precious reliquary to the convent of Poitiers. Here are the words of this beautiful hymn composed by Venantius Fortunatus for that occasion:[10]

> The Royal Banner forward goes,
> The mystic Cross refulgent glows:
> Where He, in Flesh, flesh who made,
> Upon the Tree of pain is laid.
>
> Behold! The nails with anguish fierce,
> His outstretched arms and vitals pierce:
> Here our redemption to obtain,
> The Mighty Sacrifice is slain.
>
> Here the fell spear his wounded side
> With ruthless onset opened wide:
> To wash us in that cleansing flood,
> Thence mingled Water flowed, and Blood.

[10.] English translation by Walter Kirkham Blount (d. 1717). This translation appeared in his *Office of Holy Week* (Paris, 1670).

Fulfilled is all that David told
In true prophetic song, of old:
Unto the nations, lo! saith he,
Our God hath reignèd from the Tree.

O Tree! In radiant beauty bright!
With regal purple meetly dight!
Thou chosen stem! divinely graced,
Which hath those Holy Limbs embraced!

How blest thine arms, beyond compare,
Which Earth's Eternal Ransom bare!
That Balance where His Body laid,
The spoil of vanquished Hell outweighed.

Hail wondrous Altar! Victim hail!
Thy Glorious Passion shall avail!
Where death Life's very Self endured,
Yet life by that same Death secured.

Such are the words of the *Vexilla Regis*, the hymn of Christian victory whose voice reaches us from the far-off sixth century.

2. Ireland, "Island of the Saints"

After it enlightened the kingdom of the Franks, the light of the Gospel illuminated another people, who lived in the British Isles: mysterious lands, concealed by fogs and battered by winds, where despite the arrival of the Roman gods, the local religion of the druids maintained a strong presence. The people worshipped water, the stars, and all the elements of nature. Druid meetings were held at night illuminated by the light of the moon, which was also considered to be a deity.

The first of these British lands that accepted the Gospel was Ireland, thanks to a youth, Saint Patrick (385–461), who was destined to become the national hero of that land. On his mother's side, Patrick was a relative of Saint Martin of Tours. When he was sixteen, Patrick was kidnapped by pirates and sold as a slave in Ireland, where he lived for six years as a keeper of his master's flock, suffering cold, hunger, and solitude. When he was freed and returned to his homeland, he always remembered that land and had a desire to return there to bring the Word of the Gospel to those pagans. "I hear," he sometimes exclaimed, "the voice of children not yet born calling me from Ireland."

One night Patrick had a vision in which a youth of extraordinary beauty appeared to him, who seemed to come from Ireland, with his hands full of letters: "I am your angel," he said to him, "take and read". He handed him a letter at the top of which was written "Voice of Ireland". Reading it, he had the impression of hearing the voices of many poor Irish people, who cried out to him, "We implore you, Patrick, come back among us and teach us the way of the Lord." He was moved to tears and wept and the angel disappeared.

Docile to this appeal, however, and touched by the memory of his years of slavery in which God had been his only faithful companion, Patrick explained to a monk who had just returned from Britain, Saint Germain, that he wanted to go and evangelise those islands. In 432, when Bishop Palladius, who had been sent by Pope Celestine to the Scots (who then populated Ireland) was about to die, Patrick renewed his request. Pope Celestine consecrated him as a bishop, and Patrick departed for England and then for Ireland, where for thirty years he undertook a prodigious missionary activity until his death in 461.

At that time Ireland was called Hibernia, the land of winter. Unlike the other British Isles, it had never known the yoke of Rome. The Roman legions had not trampled its ground. It was a virgin land. But it was also a land proliferated by wizards and sorcerers who, having been warned by the devil, announced that a young man would come to the island with a shaved head like that of a monk, carrying a pilgrim's staff, and that he would destroy the ancient traditions of the country. However, nothing could stop Patrick, who peacefully conquered the heart of the Irish, thanks also to a series of impressive miracles. The life of Saint Patrick was characterised by prayer and penance. When he died, the entire island had received a profound Catholic imprint that it never lost over the course of the centuries. It had such a great number of monasteries that it could legitimately be called the Island of the Saints.

Beginning in 444, the monastery of Armagh in the north of Ireland became the metropolitan see and the most important place for the ecclesial life of the country. The ascetical ideal of the Irish monks was the *peregrinatio pro Christo* or *pro Dei amore* — leaving one's homeland to spread the Gospel "overseas" in the islands and on the continent.

Daniel-Rops writes:

> "In those years, the chronicle would be filled with prodigious adventures, as monks made vows never to return to their native country in order to go everywhere and preach the Gospel, crews in ships without oars abandoned themselves to the sea in order to better abandon themselves to the will of God, and stone basins miraculously transformed into navigable ships in order to lead the saints where Providence wanted them."

> "From the western coast of Great Britain and what we call the land of the Scots, Scotland, would also arise convents from which the Gospel was spread: Bangor, in Chester, founded by Saint Comgall; and monasteries in Scotland founded by Saints Kentigern and Ninian. Further away, always further away, towards the most unknown and

terrible lands, all for Jesus Christ! Not content to have already created the abbeys of Durrow and Derry in Ireland, Saint Columba, an old monk of Clonard, embarked with twelve companions and converted the savage Picts, founding the monastery of Iona on a tiny island on the westernmost point of Scotland. Iona would become a nursery for bishops, a true Scottish metropolis, from which the good news would depart towards the Orkney Islands, the Shetlands, the Faroes, Thule — the point farthest north for the ancients — and even Iceland. To what dangers and strange adventures these daring voyages brought the monks may be seen in the fascinating legends of Saint Brendan which are still told in Britain, full of anecdotes both cheerful and terrifying, where one hears of Masses said on the back of a whale that was taken for an island, and of the gates of hell, from which the fire of the polar volcanoes came out amidst the ice… This is not merely a legend. When the Vikings discovered Iceland in the seventh century, they would find that Irish abbots were already installed there and that every island of the North Sea had its own colony of ascetics."

3. "Not Angles, Angels"

In those same years at the end of the sixth century, one day in the Roman Forum, where the slave market was held, a young monk was impressed by a group of young slaves, white-skinned slaves with blue eyes, and blond hair, in contrast to the majority of the other slaves, who were dark-skinned. "Where do they come from?" he asked. "From Britain," came the reply. "Are they Christian or pagan?" he continued. "Pagan." "And what is their nation?" "They are Angles," he was answered. "I would say rather that they are Angels," the young monk exclaimed, adding: "What a shame that the grace of God does not yet touch these beautiful foreheads." A few years later, the young monk rose to the papacy with the name of Gregory, and today he has entered into history as Gregory the Great (c.540–604).

What remained of the Roman Empire had fallen prey to devastation, but Gregory, born into a noble Roman family, wanted to give the Gospel of Christ the same conquering mission that had once belonged to the Roman Empire. He was convinced that the act of evangelisation was the primary mission of the Church, following the mandate of her Founder: "Go ye into the whole world, and preach the gospel to every creature" (Mk 16:15). Faith is not promised to all individuals but to all peoples. And so it is the peoples, the nations — not only individual people — who must be conquered for Christianity.

It was the year 596 when Gregory, who had been pope for six years, decided to entrust the task of converting England to a group of monks from his monastery on the Caelian Hill, led by their prior Augustine. Bede the Venerable has left us a detailed account of this undertaking, the great consequences of which Gregory could not foresee: it would open the path to the mission among the peoples of Germany.

In England, the island of the angels, King Ethelbert of Kent (552–616) had married a Catholic princess, Bertha of Paris, the great-granddaughter of Clovis, who was for her husband another Clothilde. The meeting of Augustine with the king was impressive: sitting under a tree, surrounded by warriors, Ethelbert saw forty Roman monks coming towards him in procession, carrying a large silver cross and the figure of Christ painted on a cloth, as hymns were sung in Gregorian chant. "The history of the Church," wrote Bossuet in regard to this scene, "has nothing more beautiful."

The personality and the arguments of Saint Augustine, united with the persuasive action of Queen Bertha, convinced the Anglo-Saxon king to grant Augustine freedom to preach in his kingdom. Only a year later, at Pentecost of the year 597, Ethelbert converted to the Catholic faith. In November of the same year, following the instructions of Pope Gregory, Augustine was consecrated as the first bishop of the Church in England by the archbishop of Arles, the papal legate. The king gave his royal palace in Canterbury to the new bishop, who made it his episcopal see and the centre of the spread of Christianity in England. On Christmas Day, Augustine baptised ten thousand Angles at one time, for which a river was needed.

The conversion of Ethelbert was memorable. After the baptism of Constantine and Clovis, there was no more important event in the annals of Christendom. Thanks to the preachers of the Gospel, the Anglo-Saxon peoples came to know not only the Catholic faith but also Roman laws, which continued to maintain their universal importance even in the places where the authority of the Roman Empire was no more than a forgotten name. The Benedictine monastery of Canterbury became a point of departure for a movement of religious and cultural organisation and unification that created a new centre of Christian civilisation in the West, which the English historian Christopher Dawson defines as "perhaps the most important event between the epoch of Justinian and that of Charlemagne." For this reason, Ethelbert can be considered the founder of the English nation, which prior to his conversion was a confused mess lacking any religious identity.

In his commentary on the Book of Job, Pope Gregory the Great traces the new horizons of the Church of Rome and compares preachers to the clouds of the firmament that irrigate and fertilise the parched clods of the earth. "The omnipotent Lord has covered the foundations of the sea with dazzling clouds," he writes, "because by means of dazzling wonders worked by preachers he has led even the extreme confines of the world to faith. Indeed, it has now penetrated the heart of almost all the peoples; behold, it has united the confines of the East and the West in one single faith; behold, the language of Britain, which did not know how to babble any language other than the barbarian one, has now begun to sing the Hebrew *Alleluia* in divine praises."

4. Saint Gregory the Great and "his women"

If conversion took place painlessly among the Franks and Anglo-Saxons, it was not so for the Visigoths of Spain. Situated at the extreme edge of Europe, Spain was the last apparently impregnable bastion of Arianism, which was professed by the Visigoth king. Saint Leander (c.549–c.601), the bishop of Seville, was the great instrument of grace for the liberation of Spain from this heresy.

In 567 King Liuvigild (525–586), a valiant German, rose to the throne of Toledo, but he was fanatically Arian, just like his wife Goiswintha, with whom he had two children, Hermenegild and Reccared. Hermenegild married a descendant of Saint Clothilde, the Frankish woman Ingund, a remarkable woman with a deep Catholic faith. Bishop Leander was connected to Ingund, and with her help he succeeded in converting one of the king's sons, Hermenegild, to the Catholic faith.

Saint Hermenegild (564–585) was the first member of the royal house of the Visigoths to abandon Arianism, embracing the Roman faith, and for this reason he is called the Clovis of Spain, but unlike the Frankish king, Hermenegild's fate was to be martyrdom. The young prince was disinherited by his father because of his conversion, and when he sought to defend himself by gathering an army, he was betrayed by his companions, conquered in battle, and decapitated at his father's orders on the vigil of Easter in the year 585. His martyrdom was not without fruit, however. One year after the martyrdom of Hermenegild, in May 586, Liuvigild died in his palace in Toledo, and his son Reccared succeeded him. He overturned his father's policy: the Catholic bishops were recalled from exile, and Saint Leander, who had become the bishop of Seville, was received at court with all the honours of a bishop. Reccared became Catholic with the support of Leander and Leander's brother, Isidore (560–636), who was himself destined to become the bishop of Seville and a saint. Thus, two Visigoth brothers, the martyr and the new king, brought about the conversion of their people thanks to the spiritual support of two other brothers who were both saints and successive bishops of Seville, Leander and Isidore.

Isidore assisted his brother Leander in the Third Council of Toledo (8 May 589) in which King Reccared solemnly abjured Arianism for himself and his people, asking to re-enter into the orthodoxy of Catholic doctrine. Thus began the Catholic history of Spain. When the Islamic tide crossed the strait of Gibraltar and Visigoth Spain crumbled, a group of Christian knights, formed in the spirit of Saint Leander and Saint Isidore, established the first nucleus of what would later be the Christian *Reconquista*.

In our narration of these events, one fact stands out: the decisive role played by women. "For the unbelieving husband," Saint Paul has said, "is sanctified by the believing wife" (1 Cor 7:14). This was never as true as in barbarian times, when we see gathered around the often violent and brutal Germanic warriors young princesses who converted them by their sweetness united to an inflexible strength in defending their own faith.

Saint Gregory the Great relied mainly on three women: the Merovingian princess Bertha (560–616), the queen of the Anglo-Saxons; the Visigoth princess Brunhilda (534–613), who became queen of the Franks; and in Italy the princess Theodelinda of Bavaria (c.570–628), the wife of King Agilulf of the Lombards. Thanks to the influence of his wife, a fervent Catholic, Agilulf had his first-born son baptised into the Catholic religion, even though he himself was an Arian. This conversion and the conversion of many great personages of the court was a fact of great importance, but it did not have such profound consequences as Clovis' baptism. Theodelinda, Bertha and Brunhilda form a triptych of female figures with whom Gregory had privileged relations, for he understood the special role of the woman in the new Christian world that was forming. Saint Bertha, queen of Kent, and Saint Theodelinda, queen of the Lombards, were canonised by the Church.

It was thanks to Gregory the Great that the Catholic faith became synonymous with Europe and remained so for almost a thousand years. The hierarchy of the Church, her unity, her sense of discipline, and her language formed the principal civil institution — the glue that held together a disintegrating society. It is enough to think of the linguistic aspect. The English writer Hilaire Belloc recalls that Europe was a jumble of infinitely varying dialects; the Latin language, in the late form in which the Church used it, was the same everywhere, and it remained extant in the rituals that differed only slightly from one province to another.

In the chaotic landscape of the sixth century, the Church was the one institution that remained on its feet, preserving the natural treasures of civilisation but above all infusing them with the new supernatural strength that was to renew it. "Gregory the Great," Msgr Umberto Benigni writes, "was neither 'the first of the popes' nor 'the last of the Romans', but he was the first of the popes and the last of the ancient Romans, he — who sent missionaries to Britain and corresponded with monks on Mount Sinai — had the strength and the opportunity to show to the entire civilised world the greatness of papal Rome within the ancient city of Rome, at the very moment at which it was disappearing forever".

5. Saint Boniface and Germany

Through the evangelisation of England, Saint Gregory prepared the way for the subsequent conversion of the Germanic nation.

If there is one European nation whose roots are eminently Christian, it is England, where, according to the historian Christopher Dawson, "it was the Church, and not the State, that paved the way for national unity by means of its general organisation, its annual synods, and its administrative tradition". But, on the other hand, there also was never an era in which the influence of Anglo-Saxon culture on the continent was greater. The apostle of Germany, Saint Boniface (673–754), was an Anglo-Saxon — "a man," writes Dawson, "who had a more profound influence on the history of Europe than any other Englishman who ever lived."

He whom history venerates under the name of Boniface was called Winfrid at his baptism: he was an Englishman from Wessex, born at Kirton in Devonshire. Like many young men of his time, he felt attracted to monastic life. During the winter of 718–719, Boniface lived in the city of Saint Peter; his future vocation would be linked to this stay in Rome.

The pope at the time was Saint Gregory II (715–732), a man of elevated mind, and of great faith, aware of the mission of the Church. Not by chance, at the moment of his election, he chose to reign as pope with the name of Gregory. His meeting with Winfrid was decisive. The impression made on him by the English saint was so great that the pontiff instantly placed in him a trust that he never lost until his death. The privilege which Winfrid demanded — to be named the papal missionary to Germany — was granted to him with enthusiasm: "You shall no longer be called Winfrid, but Boniface: he who does good!"

"When he departed for the mysterious lands where the pagan souls awaited him," writes Daniel-Rops, "Boniface was the representative of the pope, a travelling bishop without a specific see, as Augustine of England had been in the beginning, a sort of direct spokesman of Saint Peter. For his entire life, the great missionary would remain faithful to this pledge of goodness taken on the Tomb of the Apostle, asking for instruction and direction from the pope on every occasion, receiving constant support from him, in a correspondence with him that we can still read, as beautiful as the exchange between the first Pope Gregory and Saint Augustine [of Canterbury]."

The protagonists of the birth of Christian civilisation upon the ruins of the Roman Empire were a great pope, Saint Gregory the Great, along with a few religious and laity, both men and women, all of whom were animated by an ardent faith in God. Their primary motive was religious, but their faith had a profound influence in the political and social realm. The explanation of what happened is found in the words that Gregory addressed to Queen Brunhilda: "Pursue the interests of God, and God will pursue your interests" (*Letters* 11, 49). These words contain a philosophy of Providence that recalls the famous passage of the Gospel: "Seek ye therefore first the kingdom of God, and his justice, and all these things shall be added unto you" (Mt 6:33).

The promises of God are immutable: what was valid in the fifth century is also valid in our own era, which is in many ways darker than the age that witnessed the fall of the Roman Empire. What seems to be declining today is in fact not a pagan empire but the same Christian civilisation that was born and developed at that time. Yet, when men cooperate with divine grace, God intervenes in history by keeping His promises.

Radio Maria, 18 January 2012

CHAPTER VII

The prime of Christian Europe

1. Charlemagne

The history of the Church is the history of the spread of the Kingdom of God on earth, according to the mandate conferred by Jesus to the apostles: "Going therefore, teach ye all nations; baptising them in the name of the Father, and of the Son, and of the Holy Ghost, teaching them to observe all things whatsoever I have commanded you" (Mt 28:19-20). And the Gospel of Saint Mark adds: "Unto all nations the Gospel must first be preached" (Mk 13:10).

The message of salvation is not addressed only to single individuals but to nations, and the history of the Church is also the history of the response of peoples and nations to this appeal of the redeemer. Nations, like individuals, are called to baptism, and they have a vocation which comes from their baptism. The vocation of each people is to conform to the designs established for them by Divine Providence. Providence has willed the variety of nations in the unity of their common purpose, which is for them, as it is for every human person, the glory of God. The Catholic Church, the guardian of the unity of faith of the Christian nations, is also the guardian of their diversity. She is called to respect, defend, and develop the vocation of every people, their individuality, and their originality.

Christian civilisation, the fruit of the Passion of Our Lord Jesus Christ, was above all this: a family of nations, different but united by the same law and the same commandment of divine love.

The first people who responded to the divine call was the nation of the Franks, and for this reason France is called the eldest daughter of the Church.

At the Mass he celebrated at Le Bourget on 1 June 1980, John Paul II addressed this plea to the French people: "Today, in the

VII THE PRIME OF CHRISTIAN EUROPE

capital of the history of your nation, I would like to repeat these words which constitute your proud title: France, eldest daughter of the Church, are you faithful to the promises of your baptism?"

Between the fifth and sixth century, France was the outpost of the missionary expansion of the Church, above all towards the British Isles. Saint Patrick departed from the coasts of Gaul, as did Saint Augustine, the bishop of Canterbury. The monks of the British Isles who had been converted to the Gospel, from Saint Columban to Saint Boniface, would in their turn kindle the flame of faith in Europe.

But the faith of Saint Boniface was born from three centuries of missionary adventure following the baptism of Clovis, and the Englishman Boniface returned the torch of faith he had received from them, to the Frankish people. It was the bishop Boniface, in fact, who anointed Pepin, king of the Franks, in 751, in the city of Soissons. After the baptism of Clovis, this event ratified the enduring alliance between the papacy and the kingdom of France.

Pepin the Short (714–768) was the son of Charles Martel, who defeated the Arabs at Poitiers in 732 and was the founder of the dynasty. The battle of Poitiers has a significant parallel with the Battle of Lepanto. It proved to be an insurmountable barrier to Muslim ferocity, saving Christianity from Islamic domination.

Pepin's son, Charlemagne (742–814), had the honour and glory of inaugurating the Western Christian Empire, and he was the prototype of the Christian hero and Christian prince. He was first of all a warrior, who in a series of hard-fought and always victorious military campaigns extended the confines of Christendom from one end of Europe to the other. The River Ebro formed the outer border of Christendom with Muslim Spain, while the Danube was the frontier of Christendom with the pagan peoples of the East.

This border delineated the largest political entity that the world had known after the Roman Empire. After defeating the Lombards in December of the year 800, Charles went to Rome to venerate the tomb of the Prince of the Apostles. On Christmas Day, Pope Leo III placed the imperial crown on his head, exclaiming the famous phrase that was repeated three times by the people with jubilation: "To Charles Augustus, crowned by the hand of God as the great and peaceful emperor of the Romans, life and victory!"

The Holy Roman Empire that was born was not a pure and simple restoration of the Western Roman Empire, which had collapsed following the barbarian invasions. The empire was called "holy" because of its religious character and "Roman" not only because it was the heir of the ancient Roman Empire, but also because it was tied to the Roman pontiff and to Rome, the centre of Christendom.

The emperor had the mission of defending the papacy, favouring the missionary expansion of the Church, defending Catholic dogma against heresies, and procuring, in concert with the pope, peace and harmony among Christian princes. The military enterprise was accompanied by a great project of political, cultural, and religious reconstruction. The greatest collaborator of Charlemagne was Alcuin of York, an English monk who was a disciple of the Venerable Bede. Charles had met him in Italy, in Parma, and had laid out for him his great plan for the rebirth of a Christian empire. Alcuin hesitated, torn between the honour of serving the emperor and the prospect of growing old in the tranquil cell of his monastery in England. Providence had established the union of these great spirits, as often happens in history.

Under the direction of Alcuin, a centre of studies was established in the emperor's palace in Aachen: the *schola palatina* or palace school. The court of Charles became a great intellectual centre, thanks to the presence of the greatest geniuses of the time who were gathered around him. Alcuin further elaborated a programme of study that spread to all the cathedral and monastery schools of the kingdom, and which remained unchanged throughout the Middle Ages. The programme included the seven liberal arts, divided into

VII THE PRIME OF CHRISTIAN EUROPE

the *trivium* (grammar, rhetoric, and logic) and the *quadrivium* (arithmetic, geometry, astronomy, and music), which was then followed by medicine, and, at the apex of all, theology. Charlemagne placed devotion to Our Lady at the centre of the religious unity of his kingdom by having a magnificent church constructed in her honour in Aachen.

Charlemagne was an extraordinary personality who had an exalted mission. The historian Giorgio Falco describes him as follows:

> "The man attracts our sympathy with his very outward appearance: a tall stature, a robust body, a virile bearing, a happy and bright face with large and lively eyes. Disdainful of foreign customs, he dressed in the common manner of the Franks and always wore his sword; but on solemn days, in the presence of foreign ambassadors, he presented himself wearing a crown adorned with jewels and precious treasures. There was much in him of his simple and robust ancestry. His favourite food was game; his favourite leisure activities were hunting and thermal baths. He had an open mind. He spoke clearly, easily, and abundantly. He was fluent in Latin, Frankish, and Romansch, and he understood Greek although he did not speak it. Throughout his entire life he nurtured an inexhaustible passion for knowledge, so much so that he ensured that all his daughters were no less instructed than his sons in the liberal arts. During his meals he had *De Civitate Dei* and the histories of the ancients read to him, and he spent his nights with feather pen and tablet in order to learn how to write, and he exerted himself in frequent vigils."

Emperor Charles died in Aachen on the morning of 28 January 814, at the age of 72, after ruling for nearly a half-century. History relates that, prior to his death, he was at table in a seaside city of Gaul when boats from the north appeared on the horizon. They were Viking pirates, who were beginning their raids with their light hulls. Charlemagne fixed his eyes on the scene for a long time, as if having a premonition of the future, and his barons saw him weeping. *Sunt lacrimae rerum* — There are tears at the heart of things. The tears that flowed from the eyes of Charlemagne, Abbé Lemann observes, were the Christian recognition of the transience of even his magnificent empire.

Charlemagne had dedicated his entire life to unifying and extending his kingdom, but after his death it was shattered by the fratricidal struggles that broke out between his heirs. The Treaty of Verdun of 843 sanctioned the fragmentation of Europe and the emergence of its first nations, France and Germany. Since then, Europe would never again know the political unity Charlemagne had achieved at the cost of so many struggles and sacrifices.

The empire of Charlemagne may appear today a failed venture, a great hope that was not accomplished. The philosophy and theology of history invite us to take our reflections further. What characterises the history of Europe, and seems to be its vocation, as we have recalled, is unity in diversity. Its diversity was seen in its nations, languages, customs, and traditions, which in the medieval era found their equilibrium within a unified vision of the world, born from the same faith, a common law, and even from a shared cultural language, Latin, which coexisted with the nascent national languages. In addition to the papacy and the empire, the universities were another unifying element of the European culture taking shape at the end of the first millennium. The University of Pavia, for example, was founded by Charlemagne himself around the year 770, according to the tradition reported by the monastic author Notker.

With hindsight, it is clear that Charles's mission was to unite Europe politically in order to unite it culturally. Once cultural unification had taken place, the political unity dissolved, and from its ashes the European nations were born during the ninth and tenth centuries, distinct but united by a shared framework of faith and values.

In the second half of the ninth century the political unity created by Charlemagne disintegrated, and Europe fell once again into chaos. Christendom was devastated from the north by Scandinavian pirates and from the south by Saracen raiders. The former pushed into the heart of France, while the latter conquered Sicily and dominated the Mediterranean.

After sacking Bordeaux, Orléans, Reims, and Paris, the Normans, led by Rollo (845–932), a giant of a man who was more than two metres tall, arrived in Chartres and laid siege to the city. The besieged people held up the relic of the tunic of the Blessed Virgin Mary, sent by the Eastern Emperor Nicephorus to Charlemagne. The fortunes of battle were reversed, and Rollo was forced to retreat for the first time. The monk Abbo, who was in the besieged city, composed a poem in honour of this event, offering up his praises to Mary, the Liberatrix of the city: *Nec te Francus fugat, nec te Burgundus cedit, sed Regina Virgo* (O barbarian, it is not the Frank who put you to flight, nor the Burgundian to whom you yielded, but the Virgin Mary, Our Queen).

Rollo received baptism in the same year, 911, and the title of Duke of Normandy. Thanks to the help of Mary, the Normans thus became part of the family of Christian peoples, of which they would become indomitable defenders.

The inhabitants of Chartres, in order to erect a monument of eternal gratitude to Mary, constructed a cathedral in their city that was unprecedented in its beauty. The Normans, impressed by the majesty and splendour of this building, wanted to construct something similar in their capital of Rouen in Normandy.

We have a letter from 1145 in which Hugues, the archbishop of Rouen, describes the work of the labourers building the cathedral, dedicated to *Notre Dame*, saying that no one was allowed to work unless he first confessed his sins and did penance for them. Richard the Lionheart (1157–1199), king of England, ordered in his will that his heart would be preserved in the cathedral of Rouen "because of the fervent devotion that was in this place". And so it was done, while the rest of his body was buried at the feet of his father in the Abbey of Fontevrault in Anjou.

2. Britain at the time of Alfred the Great

The destiny of England in the early Middle Ages is mysterious. Why was it not conquered by Charlemagne, remaining outside the dominion of a vast Christian empire that stretched from the Ebro to the Tiber and from the Tiber to the Rhine and the Danube?

Abbé Lemann answers that the island of Britain remained free and independent because it was meant to become a refuge in the tribulations that the continent of Europe would undergo in the turbulent era which followed the death of Charlemagne.

Its geographical situation predisposed it for this providential role of asylum. The ninth and tenth centuries, which witnessed the decomposition of the empire of Charlemagne, were punctuated by wars, looting, revolts, and suffering of every sort. Great Britain appeared as a refuge: a lighthouse that shone brightly as the darkness of decadence fell upon Europe. The title "Island of the Saints" has been attributed to Ireland, but also to England, so much so that at his trial on 14 November 1581, Saint Edmund Campion (1540–1581) said to his judges before he was put to death, "In condemning us, you condemn your ancestors, priests, bishops, and sovereigns, and all those who were once the glory of England, the Island of the Saints and the most devoted daughter of the Throne of Peter."

When the Vikings invaded Britain in 870, they advanced towards the monastery of Coldingham. The abbess Ebba, who is known as

Saint Ebba the Younger, gathered her religious sisters and exhorted them to save their honour by giving them an example. After having turned a final glance towards the Virgin Mary, she took a razor and cut off her nose and upper lip. Her sisters imitated her, thus mutilating their faces one after the other in order to preserve their chastity. The next day, the Vikings arrived and found themselves before a terrible spectacle. They set the abbey on fire, and the nuns died as martyrs amidst the flames, but obtained the conversion of their executioners. Saint Etheldreda (636–679) had been a novice in the monastery of Coldingham. She was the sister of three other English saints: Ethelburga, Sesburga, and Withburga. These four sisters, all of whom were canonised by the Church, had their spiritual model in Saint Wilfrid (c.633–c.709), the great bishop. Plinio Corrêa de Oliveira considers Saint Etheldreda "one of the seeds planted by God in the history of Europe in order to give birth to the Middle Ages".

Around the same year of the martyrdom of Saint Ebba, Providence raised up in England Alfred the Great King of Wessex (849– 899), who emulated Charlemagne — he was the hero who defended the kingdom against the Vikings, who had occupied the centre and east of England. Their king Guthrum, the leader of the men who had massacred the nuns of Coldingham, was converted and had himself baptised with the name of Aethelstan. The converted Viking warriors then Christianised England, just as the Normans had Christianised France.

The father of Alfred, king of Wessex, had married Judith, the daughter of the Carolingian King Charles the Bald. Alfred therefore descended directly from Charlemagne, and the Carolingian court served as his model. He translated Saint Gregory the Great's *Pastoral Rule* and spread it throughout England, along with Saint Augustine's *Soliloquies* and the Psalter (of which Alfred personally translated the first fifty Psalms). Under Alfred's reign, the monasteries were centres of teaching where the study of the sacred scripture and the liberal arts, as well as of Latin and Christian culture, reached the highest level. Alfred the Great would be venerated as a saint, as was Saint Edward the Confessor (1043–1066) after him, the last of the Anglo-Saxon kings. The most characteristic form of Marian devotion in England dates to King Edward the Confessor: the consecration of the kingdom to the Blessed Virgin as "Mary's dowry". According to English matrimonial customs, by offering England to the Blessed Virgin as her dowry, he gave her everything he possessed, and from that time on he no longer governed in his own name but as her vassal. The English people in their turn felt proud of their identity as "Mary's dowry".

3. The epic of Covadonga

Another land, Spain, was placed like Great Britain on the western edge of Christian Europe. Beyond these lands lay the ocean.

When the apostles departed from Jerusalem, dividing up the regions of the world to evangelise them, Spain fell to the son of Zebedee, James, the brother of Saint John, whom Jesus had wanted to be with him both for the splendours of Mount Tabor as well as the anguish of the Garden of Olives.

James, called the Greater, arrived near Saragossa in the year 39. He was praying one night on the banks of the River Ebro, disappointed by the inefficiency of his preaching, when a woman of incomparable beauty appeared to him in dazzling light on a jasper pillar, surrounded by a procession of angels. He recognised her and fell prostrate before her.

According to a vision of the Venerable Maria d'Agreda recorded in her *Mystical City of God*, Mary spoke to him sweetly, saying: "Be blessed by the right hand of my son, minister of the Most High; He supports you and shows you the joy of his face." All the angels then exclaimed: "Amen." Mary continued:

"The exalted King has chosen this place so that you may erect a temple on it, where under the title of my name His own name may be magnified, and where His treasures may be communicated with abundance. He will give free course to His ancient mercies for the benefit of believers, and they will obtain them through my intercession if they ask for them with authentic confidence and pious devotion. For His part, I promise them enormous favours and my protection, because this must be my dwelling place and my inheritance. In testimony of this, this pillar surmounted by my image will remain here and will endure along with the Holy Faith until the end of time. You will start the work without delay, and after having rendered this service to Him you will depart for Jerusalem, because the Saviour desires that you sacrifice your life to Him there where He gave His for the ransom of men."

In remembrance of this visit, Our Lady left James the jasper pillar, from which *Nuestra Señora del Pilar* takes her name. Today she is the patron of Spain, and her feast day is celebrated on 12 October. James built the chapel requested of him by the heavenly visitor, and then he left Spain to become the first bishop of Jerusalem and the first martyr of the Apostolic College. The chapel built by the apostle in Saragossa later took the name of Santa Maria del Pilar. Since then this image has been an unshakeable pillar of the Catholic faith in Spain.

Venerable Maria d'Agreda further recounts that when the Blessed Mother was carried back by angels from the banks of the Ebro to Jerusalem, she obtained from the Lord that she would remain to preside over Spain, protecting its faith.

Saint James was beheaded in Jerusalem in the year 41 by the order of King Herod, but according to tradition his disciples placed his body on a ship because they were afraid of the Jews. Entrusting the task of his burial to Divine Providence, they too got aboard the boat without a helmsman. The angel of the Lord made them land safe and sound in Spain, where James's body was buried and miraculously rediscovered eight centuries later.

The history of Christian Spain is a history of martyrdom and wars fought in the name of the faith. All of Spain recalls Saint Leocadia, the virgin of Toledo who was martyred under Emperor Diocletian. Turning her serene gaze towards her companions who were weeping, she said, "Forward, soldiers of Christ! Rejoice with me that you have been judged worthy to suffer for the name of Jesus." The bishop Cixila (eighth century), in his *Life of Saint Ildefonsus* recounts that on the day of the feast of Saint Leocadia (9 December), when Saint Ildefonsus (607–667), who was the archbishop of Toledo, and the Visigoth King Recceswinth were gathered with many of the faithful in the temple erected in her honour, the slab of the tomb was raised and Leocadia appeared. She spoke to Ildefonsus with these words: "Ildefonsus, by means of you my Queen triumphs — she who resides in the heights of heaven." The archbishop, recovering from his surprise and desiring that the miracle would be known for posterity, took the king's dagger and cut off a piece of the saint's veil; he placed this relic with the king's dagger in the Church of Toledo, where it is still venerated today.

When the Roman persecutions ended, Spain was invaded by the Vandals led by Genseric. The Vandals passed into Africa and occupied it. Other barbarians, the Visigoths, occupied the Spanish peninsula. Like the Vandals, the Visigoths were Arians. Toulouse was the capital of their kingdom. They were in turn invaded by the Moors, who in 711 subjugated the Iberian Peninsula in just fifteen months, raising the Islamic flag. Their occupation lasted many centuries, but, as Abbé Lemann observes, Providence, which seems to be pleased with contrasts, assigned Spain the vocation of being an outpost against Muslim attacks.

VII THE PRIME OF CHRISTIAN EUROPE

In the hour in which everything seemed lost, a knight of royal blood named Pelayo (c.690–730) incited resistance. He gathered his few men on a high mountain in Asturias, where an image of Our Lady was venerated in a cavern, and he placed the destiny of Spain in her hands. Since then this image has been known as Santa Maria de Covadonga.

In this place, in 722, a handful of knights under the leadership of Pelayo himself defeated the Mohammedan army sent to subdue them. Tradition has it that Our Lady appeared to Pelayo and his companions at arms on the night before the battle. It was then that the *Reconquista* began with the cry of *Nuestra Señora*, a military epic against Islam that lasted for eight centuries.

After the very short reign of Pelayo's son Favilla, his general Alfonso I (739–757) took the crown and conquered part of Galicia, León, and Castile. Subsequently, Alfonso II (791–842) was a great administrator of the kingdom, to which he gave a civil and ecclesiastical structure, fixing its capital in Oviedo, which became the principal religious centre of Catholic Spain.

In this era, the blood of the martyrs was shed above all in the caliphate of Cordova, in Andalusia, by the Emir Abd al Rahman II (822–852), who resided there. Around the year 850, he forced Christians to convert to Islam. "What do you think of Jesus Christ and Mohammed?" the qadi, a Muslim judge, asked of a priest called Perfecto. The confessor of the faith replied: "Jesus Christ is the blessed God of all things. Mohammed, your alleged prophet, is one of the seducers of whom the Gospel speaks, who must plunge their followers into the abyss of hell." He was immediately put to death, and the same fate befell a merchant called Juan, who died after receiving five hundred blows of the whip.

This double news shook the Christian community. Some monks came down from the mountains to proclaim their faith in the public squares of Cordova. The most ardent of them was Isaac, from the monastery of Tabanos, who was put to death in 851. His body was hung in a public place to expose him to the contempt of the crowd. But far from frightening the other monks, this treatment aroused in them a greater audacity. Every martyrdom, the historian Ivan Gobry recalls, encouraged the testimony of other disciples of Christ to become martyrs in their turn.

On 16 September there was a terrible execution of two monks from the East, Rogelio and Servideo, one an elderly man, the other in his youth. They entered the mosque right in the middle of Friday prayers and preached Jesus Christ. First their hands and feet were cut off, and then their heads.

Under Abd al-Rahman II a council was held at which all the archbishops and bishops of the south of Spain gathered. The caliph tolerated Christians on the condition that they recognised Islamic authority, and he wanted the bishops to condemn all Christians who were criticising the religion of Mohammed and thus incurring martyrdom. Martyrdom was not itself disparaged, nor could it have been: it remains one of the peaks of Christian spirituality, but the bishops prohibited Christians from seeking it out, and they condemned Saint Eulogius, who urged public witness against bishops who were tempted by compromise. Plinio Corrêa de Oliveira observes: "Saint Eulogius went through the hard test of being condemned by a synod of bishops, but despite his suffering he considered it his duty to resist an unjust condemnation made by evil bishops, and by behaving in this way he actually gave us an example of authentic love for the Church. Obeying God rather than men, he obeyed the Church, as was authoritatively recognised later."

The Christians, however, did not cease to give witness to their faith, and the caliph, seized with rage, gave the order to burn the bodies of the martyrs exposed on the gallows. He was then struck by apoplexy and died without recovering his ability to speak. His successor Moham followed the same policy and a new legion of witnesses to Christ enriched the martyrology. We recall Saint Fandila, Saint Colomba, and Saint Abbondius who was a parish priest in

VII THE PRIME OF CHRISTIAN EUROPE

Sierra Morena who was condemned to death, thrown to the dogs, and devoured by them on 11 July 854.

The year 859 saw the execution of Saint Eulogius, the biographer and defender of all the preceding martyrs. He had been elected bishop of Toledo but was not able to be consecrated because he was beheaded. He deserves to be named the patron saint of the twenty-first century martyrs of Islam.

Meanwhile, in northern Spain, under the long reign of Alfonso the Chaste (791–842), the famous pilgrimage to Santiago di Compostela took hold, following the discovery of the relics of Saint James in 813. The popular tradition named the place of the discovery Compostela: *campus stellae*, the field of the star. Bishop Theodomir discovered in that place a tomb which contained three bodies. One of the three had a severed head and an inscription: "Here lies Jacobus, the son of Zebedee and Salome." Alfonso II ordered the construction of a temple over the place, where Benedictine monks established their residence in 893. Thus began the first pilgrimages to the tomb of the apostle, first from the Asturias and Galicia and then from all of Europe.

In the twelfth century, a cry of fury rose from Islam when Spain, a conquered land, was being lost. A holy war was proclaimed, and the innumerable tribes which populated North Africa crossed the straits of Gibraltar, invading the Iberian Peninsula. Up until then the Christians of Spain had fought alone, with the sole help of Saint James, who had been seen participating in bloody fights against the Muslims, killing not a few of them with his own hands. Hence he was given the nickname *Santiago Matamoros*: Saint James the killer of the Moors.

But this time the Church intervened. Pope Innocent III (1160–1216) made an appeal to all Christendom. Sixty thousand knights, who came from France, Italy and Germany, reached the Pyrenees, enlisting under the banners of the three Catholic kings of Navarre, Aragon and Castile, and Portugal. From the Sierra Morena the

Christian army swooped down on the Arabs, dispersing them. It was the memorable Battle of Las Navas de Tolosa of 16 July 1212. Thanks to this victory the process of unification of the Christian kingdoms began which led to the formal union of Castile and Aragon through the marriage of Ferdinand II of Aragon and Isabella of Castile. The Blessed Mother, from the back of the cavern of Covadonga, had directed this epic battle, in which many heroes took part — like the king of Castile who, although he was already paralysed, had himself carried on a litter to the battlefield, where he faced and defeated the terrible Al-Manzar.

In this gigantic struggle, the epitome of Spanish valor was the *Cid Campeador*, Rodrigo Díaz de Vivar (c.1048–1099). *Cid* means "Lord" in the Arabic language, and *campeador* means "hero without equal", captain *par excellence*. This nickname was given by the Moors themselves to Rodrigo of Castile, who after conquering five of their kings was recognised as their sovereign.

4. The Christian empire at the dawn of the year 1000

On Christmas Day 496, Clovis was baptised, and on Christmas Day 800, Charlemagne was crowned emperor.

But the history of Christendom knows another happy Christmas Day: that of the year 951, when King Otto of Saxony (912–973), the first to have this name, married princess Adelaide of Bourgogne (931–999) near Pavia. Adelaide had been persecuted and placed in prison by Berengarius II of Friuli, the lord of the kingdom of Italy, because she had refused to marry his son. She was liberated by Otto I, married him, and they had three children. Otto was destined to become an emperor and Adelaide a saint. Earthly glory was married to supernatural virtue.

In 962, Pope John XIII invited the German king and his wife to Rome to kneel before the tomb of the Prince of the Apostles, and

VII THE PRIME OF CHRISTIAN EUROPE

there, amidst the acclamations of the Roman people, he placed the imperial crown on their heads. By this ceremony the empire was transferred from the Franks to the Germans. It marked the birth of what would be called the "Holy Roman Empire of the German Nation".

Holiness surrounded the throne of Otto. Saint Adelaide was his wife. Saint Matilde (c.890–968) was his mother, who after living as a widow went to the Abbey of Quedlinburg which she had founded. Saint Bruno I (925–955), the archbishop of Cologne, was his brother. Bruno was the regent of the kingdom during the second expedition of Otto I to Italy. A few decades later, his successor on the imperial throne, Henry II (973–1024), and his wife Cunigunde would be saints.

Adelaide formed her son Otto II (c.955–983) both spiritually and politically, and after his death also her grandson Otto III (980–1002). The regency was held by Adelaide until the young king was declared to have attained majority in 994. Otto III placed the idea of the *Renovatio Imperii* at the centre of his reign. The young emperor, the son of Otto II and the empress Theophanu, united the Germanic and Byzantine traditions: the imperial conception of Charlemagne together with that of Justinian. Beginning in 999, he resided with his court in his sumptuous palace on the Aventine Hill. Referring to himself, he wrote: "I, Otto, Roman, Saxon and Italian, Servant of the Apostles, by divine grace Emperor Augustus of the World." On the day of Pentecost in the year 1000, Otto III, who had only recently been crowned in Rome, ordered Charlemagne's burial place to be found and visited his remains in the ancient palace chapel of Aachen.

On 1 January 1001, Duke Wajk, the son of Grand Prince Geza of Hungary, who had been baptised with the name of Stephen, became the first king of Hungary (1001–1038). He received the crown from the hands of Pope Sylvester II, who granted him the title of *Rex Apostolicus* for having made Hungary a Christian nation.

Stephen consecrated his kingdom to the Blessed Virgin. After his death, he was raised to the altars as patron saint of his nation and as the Holy Protector of Hungary. Polish Duke Mieszko and Saint Stephen of Hungary each made a gift of their nations to the pope. In a miniature of the time, four women are depicted bowing down to the pope: Rome (Italy), Gaul, Germany, and *Sclavinia* (the nation of the Slavs).

The tenth century had opened with the baptism of Rollo of Normandy and had seen the start of the Christianisation of the Scandinavian peoples beginning with Denmark, as well as the evangelisation of the Slavs, Bohemians, Poles, and Hungarians. A new Christendom was taking shape at the dawn of the new millennium, when Otto III died at the age of only 22, at Paterno, near Mount Soratte northeast of Rome, on 23 January 1002.

He was succeeded on the throne of Germany by another saint, his cousin Henry III. He had to fight the hordes which arrived from the East and which continually attacked the empire. He raised a large army to respond to the aggression of these barbarians. He fought many wars and did so as a Catholic hero who had the spirit of faith, trusting more in supernatural help than in his own natural powers. He asked God for the strength to win his battles, and God showed Saint Henry how much he appreciated his prayers by intervening in a miraculous way on more than one occasion. When his army and a pagan army were face to face, the enemy fled in fear for no apparent reason. In order to terrorise the saint's enemies, God had showed them an angel at the head of a host of martyrs.

The Lord appreciated the soldiers' prayers so much that on this occasion he granted them the victory without even having to fight. And with this victory, the pagan forces of the East had to retreat, and paganism lost its momentum for expansion.

But a danger still threatened Christendom: the presence of the followers of Arduin of Ivrea (955–1015) in southern Italy. Arduin pursued a supremacy that led him to clash with the Church and the

VII THE PRIME OF CHRISTIAN EUROPE

empire. So Saint Henry, with the support of many bishops in Italy, invaded the territory of Arduin, defeated him, and then went to Rome where he offered homage to Pope Benedict VIII (†1024), who crowned him as emperor of the Holy Roman Germanic Empire. In a ceremony carried out with great splendour, he gave Saint Henry a golden globe studded with pearls, which represented the power of the emperor over the whole world. But Saint Henry did not keep this treasure for himself. He showed his love for the Church by offering the precious gift to the abbot of Cluny, Saint Odilo.

The role of Saint Henry was also decisive in the conversion of King Stephen of Hungary, to whom he offered his sister in marriage, Blessed Gisela of Bavaria (980–1065). She married Stephen and brought him to faith in Christ. But the name of Saint Henry cannot be separated from that of his wife, Cunigunde, who was another great saint. Both of them made a vow of chastity, offering their marriage to the Lord, and today they await the day of resurrection together in the Cathedral of Bamberg, which they constructed.

After Saint Boniface and Saints Cyril and Methodius, Saint Adalbert (956–997) is the great figure of the Christianisation of the peoples of Central and Eastern Europe. Born in Bohemia, he abandoned his Slavic name Vojtech in order to take the name of his protector, Archbishop Adalbert. He became a monk and a priest, and in 983 he became bishop of Prague. He died martyred by the pagans of Prussia near Danzig on 23 April 997. A similar fate befell the monk Saint Bruno of Querfurt and his 18 companions, who were martyred, according to the historical record, on the border of Lithuania and Russia. Saint Adalbert was buried in Gniezno. He was venerated throughout Poland and Hungary, and above all in Bohemia, where he became a symbol of national identity.

The conversion of the Russian people took place in 998, with the baptism of Saint Vladimir I (c.956–1015), who became Grand Prince of Kiev around 980. From the beginning of the eleventh century, the term Rus (*Russkaya Zemlye*) designated the territories subject to the princes of Kiev, the Ukrainian city of great strategic importance as the point of confluence between the Baltic, the Byzantine Empire, and the Abassid Caliphate. The baptism of Vladimir in 988 brought about the conversion of Russia. *The Rus' Primary Chronicle*, written in the twelfth century, tells of this conversion, which was followed by a great diffusion of Byzantine culture. A metropolitan see was erected in Kiev, which became one of the greatest cities of Eastern Europe.

At the dawn of the year 1000, the borders of Christendom were expanding both east and north. Europe experienced great demographic growth, and as a result economic growth, but above all a spiritual growth, so much so that a chronicler, Rudolph the Bald, speaks of a "white mantle of churches" that seemed to cover it.

The year 1000 seemed to inaugurate an era of new youthfulness for Europe. The historian Roberto Sabatino Lopez recalls a couplet, written in the tenth century, in a language that is no longer Latin but is not yet identifiable as one of the modern Romance languages: *L'alba part umet mar atra sol; poy pasa bigil, mira clar tembras* ... (Dawn brings the sun to the dark sea; then it crosses the great hill, the darkness clears ...).

The Church, writes Plinio Corrêa de Oliveira, "thus spread its hierarchical structure over all of Europe and, from the mists of Scotland to the slopes of Vesuvius, dioceses, monasteries, cathedral churches, convents, and parishes flourished, and around them the flock of Christ ... By virtue of these human energies, revitalised by grace, kingdoms and noble lineages were born, as well as courteous customs and just laws, congregations and chivalry, scholarship and the universities, the Gothic style and the minstrels' songs."

These are our roots. But this is also our future, because nothing is impossible, with the help of God, for those who love the Church and Christian civilisation and fight for it.

Radio Maria, 15 February 2012

CHAPTER VIII
The reform of the Church of the year 1000

1. The plagues of the Church in the eleventh century

Light and shadow intertwine in the history of the Church, but she is always divinely assisted by the Holy Ghost, who transforms the shadows into light and guides everything towards the good.

The fact that there is a supernatural direction of history by which good always prevails over evil does not however erase the tragic dimension of the life of men, of peoples, and of the Church herself, in whose existence good and evil, truth and error, oppose one another and fight against one another.

This struggle is at times internal — it may happen, as described in the famous speech of Paul VI, that the smoke of Satan enters into the temple of God, that the abomination infiltrates the holy place.

This is what happened at the end of the first millennium. The coronation of Charlemagne was an extraordinary event: it was the birth of that Christian civilisation in which, according to Leo XIII, "the philosophy of the Gospel governed the nations" (Encyclical *Immortale Dei*, 1 November 1885).

And yet, beginning with the end of the empire of Charlemagne (888), in the tumultuous era in which the first Christian nations were formed, a time came which Cardinal Baronius in his *Annals* calls "the age of iron" — leaden and gloomy because of its barbarism and its widespread evil.

The great Oratorian historian warns his readers not to be scandalised if they come to see the abomination within the very sanctuary of the Church, but rather to reflect on the divine power during that age which prevented the complete ruin of ecclesiastical society.

It was a sad page in the history of the Church, which witnessed 45 popes and antipopes succeed each other between 882 and 1046, of whom 15 were deposed and 14 were assassinated, imprisoned or exiled. It is enough to recount that one pope, Stephen VI (or VII) (896–897), exhumed the cadaver of his predecessor Formosus (891–896), which had already lain buried for nine months in the atrium of Saint Peter's Basilica and held a full canonical trial of the deceased pontiff, over which he presided in the Lateran Basilica. The body of Pope Formosus was carried before a council of priests and bishops of his party, still wearing his pontifical vestments. They succeeded in placing him on a throne, and a deacon responded to

VIII THE REFORM OF THE CHURCH OF THE YEAR 1000

the accusations against him. At the end of the macabre spectacle, Stephen condemned the memory of Formosus to perpetual infamy and declared all the acts of his pontificate null. After stripping him of his vestments, he had the three fingers with which Formosus had given the papal blessing cut from the corpse and then his miserable remains were thrown into the Tiber. Following this, the faction that opposed Pope Stephen swore an oath against him and had him imprisoned and strangled. After this episode, the clergy and the Roman people were divided into two parties, the Formosians and the anti-Formosians, and for many years thereafter these two factions fought for power.

Did the Holy Ghost abandon the Church during this period? Certainly not: in this dark period in which unworthy representatives ascended to the papal throne, the Holy Ghost assisted the Church, just as He assisted her when, as Cardinal Hergenröther writes, "in the entire first half of the tenth century, everything seemed to be thrown out of its normal state; the corruption of the age appeared to inundate the Church, and the discipline of the Church seemed to be annihilated."

Two plagues desolated the Church between the tenth and eleventh century: simony and the moral dissolution of the clergy.

The term and concept of "simony" derive from a sacrilegious offer made to the apostles by Simon Magus (Acts 8:12-24), a Samaritan man of the time who was known for his magic. He offered money to the apostles in order to obtain from them the power to impose hands on Christians and confer the gifts of the Holy Ghost. According to the definition given by Saint Thomas Aquinas, simony is "the premeditated or deliberate intention to buy or sell something spiritual or pertaining to the spiritual" (*Summa Theologica* II-IIae, q.100). The Church has always condemned buying or selling for a monetary price a material thing connected to a spiritual good. Saint Gregory the Great testifies in his correspondence about these abuses in the sixth century, and he described simony as heresy (*simoniaca haeresis*). In the tenth and eleventh centuries simony was widespread. The purchasing of ecclesiastical offices was often tied to the problem of investitures, that is, the granting of offices and ecclesiastical benefices by secular authorities. It was a consequence of the secular powers intervening in the affairs of the Church and, more generally, it was the problem of the relationship between Church and State.

The other grave problem of those times was *nicolaitism*, a term used to condemn the abuse of the cohabitation of bishops and priests with women, which penetrated the Church. The practice takes its name from the Nicolaitists, identified in the Book of Revelation in the letters to the Churches of Ephesus and Pergamum (Rev 2:6, 14-16) as "false apostles" who claimed to have the gifts of a prophetic charism and practiced immorality.

Saint Irenaeus says that they were the disciples of Nicholas, one of the first seven deacons of the Church in Jerusalem (Acts 6:5-6) and considers them to be a branch of false gnosis. In the eleventh and twelfth centuries the term was used to stigmatise infractions against the rule of clerical celibacy. The moral dissolution was not limited to the concubinage of priests, but unfortunately it had one of its most disgraceful expressions in the "cancer of sodomitic infection", homosexuality among priests and religious which, Saint Peter Damian writes in his *Liber Gomorrhanus*, raged "like a bloody beast in the fold of Christ".

Even in periods of doctrinal and moral crisis in the Church, the truth of Christ and his law remains immutable, and the Church continues to be holy in her dogmas, her sacraments, and in the souls whom the Holy Ghost fills with his grace.

The Church is not only occasionally under the influence of the Holy Ghost — she is constantly under the influence of the Holy Ghost, who acts both through ecclesiastical authority as well as through the gifts poured out on all of the Church's members. And if it is true that the principal beneficiaries of this assistance are the ministers of the *ecclesia docens*, the historian must not forget that in reality the assistance of the Holy Ghost is expressed above all in holiness, which, as Dom Guéranger explains, is distributed by the Holy Ghost to all the members of the Mystical Body.

2. The Italian reformers

In the eleventh century, the Holy Ghost drew from the monasteries the spiritual resources that the Church needed to emerge from this profound crisis. In those ages there was a prodigious growth and multiplication of abbeys and convents that spread the spirit of the Gospel throughout Europe. The roots of this flowering lay in the work of Saint Benedict of Nursia, of whom we have already spoken.

The Benedictine family always proceeds on the straight path through the centuries, Dom Guéranger remarks, but from the trunk of this mighty tree have sprung four branches, which still remained attached to the trunk and which were granted vitality and fecundity by the Holy Ghost for many centuries: the Camaldolese founded by Romuald, Cluny founded by Odilo, Vallombrosa founded by Giovanni Gualberto, and Citeaux founded by Robert of Molesmes.

Saint Romuald (c.952–1027), the son of Sergio, the Duke of Ravenna, was about twenty years old in 972 when he entered the Benedictine monastery of Saint Apollinare in Classe in order to expiate a crime committed by his father, who had challenged his brother to a duel and killed him. Romuald, who was seventeen years old at the time, had been a witness to the duel but also acted as his father's second. He was deeply affected by this experience, and as a result he turned to the Lord and founded the Camaldolese Order in Tuscany in 1012, whose constitutions were written by Blessed Rudolf around the year 1080, more than 50 years after the death of Saint Romuald.

In 1038, a disciple of Saint Romuald, Saint Giovanni Gualberto (985/995–1073) founded the Vallombrosian order in the town of

Vallombrosa in Tuscany, not far from the town of Camaldoli; these monks also lived a cenobitic life. Like Romuald, Gualberto was also of noble birth, and he became a monk following the extraordinary events that occurred after he forgave the man who killed one of his brothers. Giovanni Gualberto and his followers in Vallombrosa were among the protagonists of the struggle against simoniacal clergy, which resulted in the deposition of the bishop of Florence, Pietro Mezzabarba, by means of the trial by fire undergone by the Vallombrosian monk Pietro Igneo.

The spirit of reform was further manifested in Saint Peter Damian (1007–1072), the abbot of the monastery of Fonte Avellana, who was later created Cardinal of Ostia by Pope Stephen IX. Born in Ravenna, a disciple of Saint Romuald, Peter Damian went to the hermitage of Fonte Avellana, which he made into a centre of austere and penitent spirituality, in contrast to the lax practices of the clergy of his time. During the pontificate of Leo IX, he composed the *Liber Gomorrhanus*, in which he exposed the faults of the clergy, beginning with the scourge of homosexuality. He sent this work to the pope and invited him to reprimand this grave evil. In the face of the profound crisis that the Church was suffering, obeying the pope's wishes, in 1057 Peter Damian left his monastery and accepted his appointment as cardinal-bishop of Ostia, thus working with greater commitment and responsibility in the difficult undertaking of the reform of the Church.

Benedict XVI spoke of Saint Peter Damian in the general audience of 9 September 2009, saying that he was "a monk through and through, with forms of austerity which to us today might even seem excessive. Yet, in that way he made monastic life an eloquent testimony of God's primacy and an appeal to all to walk towards holiness, free from any compromise with evil. He spent himself, with lucid consistency and great severity, for the reform of the Church of his time. He gave all his spiritual and physical energies to Christ and to the Church, but always remained, as he liked to describe himself, *Petrus ultimus monachorum servus* (Peter, the lowliest servant of the monks)."

A great author of the twentieth century, Plinio Corrêa de Oliveira, recalls that Saint Peter Damian spread the use of the penitential practice known as the "discipline", a sort of whip formed by knotted cords. Today it is perhaps difficult for us to understand this practice. But spreading it, Professor Corrêa de Oliveira writes, was one of the great services Saint Peter Damian did for the Church, because in doing so he spread the spirit of penance.

The spirit of penance "is much more than physical pain or the act of humility that is tied to the use of a specific instrument like the discipline. The spirit of penance is the understanding and adherence to the general principles on which the idea of penance is founded." What are these principles? Corrêa de Oliveira continues:

> "Man is born with original sin and so he must fight against the instincts and passions which stem from it. Man is a sinner, and sin is an offence against the justice of the Divine Majesty which requires reparation. This reparation ought to be a suffering proportionate to the offence committed. Often this offence is an illicit pleasure that has not been given up. Just as a thief who has stolen money is bound to return it, so the one who has enjoyed stolen pleasures he did not have the right to before God must also make restitution, in order to restore balance on the scales of Divine Justice. A person has a spirit of penance if he understands the gravity of his sins. But one can also do penance even without having a specific sin to expiate. Even in this case, penance is useful for struggling against negative inclinations of the flesh and against the tendency to rebellion of human pride.

> Modern man abhors penance, and even more the spirit of penance. Most films, novels, and environments are a

thousand miles away from the notion of penance. Instead, invitations to exacerbate pride and sensuality seem to be omnipresent. By spreading the use of the discipline, the hair shirt, and other instruments of penance, Peter Damian has done us a favour, because he has helped us to form a penitential mentality and to recall that we must fight against our wicked inclinations."

3. The spirit of Cluny

The deepest monastic reform was the Reform of Cluny, which was destined to go down in history because of its great and lasting work of religious renewal of the Church.

The Abbey of Cluny was founded on 11 September 910 in Bourgogne by William the Pious, Duke of Aquitaine, who gave "to the holy Apostles Peter and Paul what he possessed in Cluny" so that a monastery would be erected there, and the monks who gathered there lived according to the Rule of Saint Benedict. The Duke entrusted the abbey's fate to Berno (910–926), a man of great virtue, who brought a group of monks to the new monastery who were inspired by the ancient Benedictine traditions. Beginning with Berno, there was a series of holy abbots in Cluny who spread their spirit throughout all of Christendom, transforming the men and institutions of the Middle Ages.

Blessed Berno was succeeded by his brother monk Saint Odo, who was abbot from 926 to 942. Odo travelled continually in order to spread and restore the Benedictine Rule. In 931 in Rome, Pope John XI took the monastery under his protection, giving Odo every faculty to spread the Cluniac reforms "during times in which almost all the monasteries are unfaithful to their Rule". Odo's biographer comments that in a single monk the various virtues were found which were all too rare in other monasteries: "Jesus, in His goodness, drawing from the various monastic gardens, formed little corners of heaven from whose fountains the hearts of the faithful were watered."

Saint Odo nourished a particular devotion to the mystery of the transformation of the bread and wine into the Body and Blood of Christ, and he deplored that this "most holy mystery of the Body of the Lord, in which the entire salvation of the world consists," was in his time celebrated negligently by priests, as unfortunately also happens today. Benedict XVI recalled Saint Odo on 2 September 2009 with these words: "Saint Odo was a true spiritual guide both for the monks and for the faithful of his time. In the face of the 'immensity of the vices' widespread in society, the remedy he strongly advised was that of a radical change of life, based on humility, austerity, detachment from ephemeral things and adherence to those which are eternal."

The charter of the foundation of Cluny gave the abbot the right to choose his successor. Thus Odo designated Aymard (942–954), who was succeeded by Saint Majolus (954–994). Born in the same year that Cluny was founded, Majolus held the post of abbot for forty years in the second half of the tenth century, until 994 when he died at the age of 84. Then, from 994 to 1109, a span of 115 years, Cluny had only two abbots: Saint Odilo, who governed Cluny for 55 years (994–1049), and Saint Hugo, who was abbot for 60 years (1049–1109). This continuity, along with the wisdom and holiness of the two abbots, was, as the historian Ivan Gobry observes, the primary cause of the prodigious flourishing of the order.

Saint Odilo, to whom we owe the feast of the commemoration of All Souls on 2 November, was also the inspiration for the "movement of peace and the truce of God" which characterised Christian spirituality between the tenth and eleventh centuries. Saint Hugo brought the abbey to the apex of its splendour, thanks to the relations he maintained with princes and sovereigns and the support he enjoyed from the popes who came out of the abbey under his governance: Blessed Urban II (1088–1099) and his successor Paschal II (1099–1118). Hugo also erected the magnificent church at Cluny which at the time was the largest in the world: 45 metres high and 180 metres long, with five naves, two transepts, and seven apsidal chapels.

At Cluny, Benedict XVI recalled in his audience of 11 November 2009, there was a desire to emphasise the central role of the liturgy in Christian life:

> "The Cluniac monks dedicated themselves with love and great care to the praying of the Liturgical Hours, to the singing of the Psalms, to processions as devout as they were solemn, and above all, to the celebration of Holy Mass. They promoted sacred music, they wanted architecture and art to contribute to the beauty and solemnity of the rites; they enriched the liturgical calendar with special celebrations such as, for example, at the beginning of November, the Commemoration of All Souls; and they strengthened the devotion to the Virgin Mary. Great importance was given to the liturgy because the monks of Cluny were convinced that it was participation in the liturgy of Heaven. And the monks felt responsible for interceding at the altar of God for the living and the dead, given large numbers of the faithful who were insistently asking them to be remembered in prayer."

"What is the liturgy?" Charlemagne asked his wise minister and chaplain Alcuin one day. "The liturgy," the monk replied, "is the joy of God!" Dom Gérard Calvet, the founder of the Benedictine monastery of Le Barroux, explains that the liturgy is the joy of God because it is the public worship which his Only Begotten Son, the Eternal Priest, offers to Him, and the priest who celebrates the Mass acts *in persona Christi* and makes the sacrifice of the Cross present on the altar in an unbloody manner. The liturgy, Dom Guéranger affirms, is also the "joy of the people", that is, the joy of men who have become sons of God, because men are made for God, to go to God; they have need of redemption, of holiness, in order to rediscover or maintain contact with God who is holy. It is the liturgy which procures this. "In it, the Holy Ghost worked the artistic miracle of concentrating, eternalising, and spreading throughout the entire Body of Christ the unalterable fullness of the redemptive work, all of the supernatural riches of the Church's past, of her present, and of her future."

In the abbey of Cluny and in the monasteries that depended on it, the life of the monks was configured as a continuous preparation for the judgment of God. The monks, however, did not isolate themselves from the world for their own individual salvation, but rather for the salvation of the entire society and the glory of God. The monastery of Cluny thus became a real island of prayer in the midst of the tumultuous medieval society.

Cluny introduced other important innovations into Christianity.

- Every abbey was strictly tied to the "mother" abbey, whose abbot ruled over all of them. He was elected by the monks of Cluny, but he was head of the entire family which depended on Cluny. The Order of Cluny presented itself as the first religious order in the history of the Church, understood as a complex of religious houses that had the same rule and depended on the same superior.

- The monastery of Cluny and the communities dependent on it were recognised as exempt from the jurisdiction of the local bishops and were placed directly under the jurisdiction of the Roman pontiff. This involved a special bond with the See of Peter, and the ideals of purity and fidelity which the Cluniac reform intended to pursue were able to spread rapidly thanks to the protection and encouragement of the popes.

- Furthermore, the abbots were elected without any interference from the secular authorities, unlike what happened in other places. This gave prestige not only to the monastery of Cluny but also to the papacy in relation to the secular powers that were growing in strength at that time.

The monastic reform of Cluny extended rapidly in Italy, Spain, and England. At the beginning of the twelfth century, when Cluny was at the height of its powers, the congregation included about twelve hundred monasteries, of which nine hundred were in France. Through monastic channels, important practices and devotions developed and spread: the evening chanting of the *Salve Regina*, devotion to Mary under the title *Mater Misericordiae*, the Little Office of the Blessed Virgin Mary, the Mass in her honour on Saturdays, the consecration of oneself as the slave the Virgin Mary, and also a fervent devotion to the angels who, according to what is reported, mingled their voices with the voices of the monks in the praises of God that rose ceaselessly from these islands of sanctity.

4. Saint Gregory VII

One of the great services that the monks rendered to the Church was assuming the papacy. Between 1057 and 1118, the See of Saint Peter was occupied by five popes who came from Benedictine monasteries: Stephen IX (1057–1058), Saint Gregory VII (1073–1085), Blessed Victor III (1086–1087), Blessed Urban II (1088–1099) and Paschal II (1099–1118). At this point we should stop to consider Saint Gregory VII, born Hildebrand of Sovana (c.1020–1085), who was also the greatest reformer of his time and

VIII THE REFORM OF THE CHURCH OF THE YEAR 1000

one of the greatest popes in history. He succeeded five popes who before him and with his help fought for what became known as the "Gregorian Reform". But none of his predecessors met with either the successes or the difficulties of Gregory VII.

Hildebrand, despite the opposition of the German and Lombard bishops and his own reluctance, was elected to the papal throne on 29 April 1073, when he was fifty years old. This is how he expressed himself as soon as he was elected:

> "I want you to know, dearest brothers — as many of you do — that we have been put in such a place so as to be constrained, willingly or unwillingly, to announce truth and justice to all the peoples, above all to the Christian people, because so the Lord has said: cry out, do not tire of shouting, lift your voice like a trumpet and announce to my people their crimes."

The new pope confronted the evils of his time head-on. A few months after his election, in 1074, Gregory convened a Council in Rome and had two important decrees approved: the first against priests who transgressed against the law of celibacy, and the second against simony. He then sent legates and letters everywhere, ordering bishops to hold councils to promulgate these decrees and ensure their observance. In a second Council in 1075 he condemned the lay investiture of bishops.

For Gregory the secular authorities were the primary ones responsible for the religious and moral decadence of the clergy, and there was a close link between simony and the politics of investiture. The public authorities (emperor, kings, dukes and counts) were the ones who appointed bishops, imposing their choice, and at times they also appeared to create them, giving them the crosier or the ring, the signs of their religious offices. The objective of Gregory was to restore the dignity and independence of the episcopate, and to reject lay investiture by the emperor or other secular powers.

King Henry IV, the clergy of Germany and Lombardy rebelled against Gregory, and the pope ordered Henry to appear in Rome on a given date, with the threat of excommunication if he failed to do so. Henry then convoked a synod at Worms, and he made an agreement with the prefect of Rome, Leucio, to dismiss Gregory. On Christmas Eve 1075, Leucio entered with his soldiers into the Basilica of Saint Mary Major, where the pope was celebrating Mass. They tore him from the altar, wounding him in the head, and took him prisoner. However, a few hours later the people liberated the pontiff. Gregory convened a new Council (1076) in which he solemnly excommunicated Henry and declared that the subjects of Germany and Italy were released from their oath of fidelity to him He wrote to the German princes not to abuse the excommunication of the king but rather to seek to make him repent.

The papal ruling was a terrible blow for the cause of Henry in Germany: many of the nobles subject to him rebelled and convoked a Diet to appoint his successor. Henry therefore, seeing the danger, went down to Italy to reconcile with the pope. Gregory had left Rome in order to participate in the Diet of Augsburg. From Mantova he went to Canossa, to the castle of Countess Matilda of Tuscany, to whom he was related. It was January. At first Gregory refused to receive Henry, but Henry arrived at the castle, walking barefoot in the snow, wearing a tunic of raw wool. The pope did not trust such a sudden repentance, but Countess Matilda and Abbot Hugo of Cluny implored the pope not to refuse the pleas of a penitent. On 28 January 1077, after three days of waiting, Henry was admitted to the presence of the pope, pardoned, and absolved of the excommunication.

About seven centuries after Emperor Theodosius had knelt as a penitent before Bishop Ambrose of Milan, a new emperor knelt before the religious authority of the Church. But the repentance

VIII THE REFORM OF THE CHURCH OF THE YEAR 1000

of Henry IV, unlike that of Theodosius, was not sincere. The sovereign did not remain faithful to his promises and took up arms against Rudolph of Swabia, who had in the meantime been elected emperor in his stead by the German princes.

Gregory VII reacted firmly by reclaiming papal authority. He summarised his position in the *Dictatus Papae*, a collection of sentences which show the relations that ought to exist between the Holy Roman Empire and the papacy. The second proposition affirms that only the monarchy of the Roman pontiff "can rightly be called universal". This universality refers to the spiritual realm. The pope did not have any pretence of governing the empire directly, but he defended the right to exercise a decisive influence on society. According to Gregory, Peter had been constituted "sovereign over the kingdoms of the world" and to him God "has subjected all the principalities and all the powers of the earth, giving him the power to bind and loose in heaven and on earth". Kings and emperors are not exempt from the divine and natural law, to which all men are subject, and of which the Church is the guardian. This principle continues to have its value even in an era like our own in which the ancient sovereigns have been replaced by modern parliaments, with even more absolute and arbitrary demands than those at the time of Gregory VII.

A war followed between those who were faithful to the emperor and those who served the pope. Gregory found support in Matilda of Tuscany (1046–1115), an extraordinary woman of Lombard lineage. Matilda had married Godfrey of Lorraine, called the Hunchback, who was assassinated in 1076. After the death of her mother she possessed sole governance of her vast State, which she donated to Gregory because she had no heirs. This was an open challenge to the emperor, given the rights that the sovereign boasted of holding over her, both as a feudal lord and as a close relative.

Henry IV convened a Council in Brixen at which he had the pope deposed, and he decreed that Matilda was deposed and banned from the empire. The emperor then went down to Rome and besieged the pope at Castel Sant'Angelo. Gregory was declared deposed, and the antipope Clement was solemnly enthroned in his place. On Easter Sunday (31 March), Henry along with his wife Bertha received the imperial crown from the antipope, but the sacking of the city by the Normans provoked the reaction of the people who, stirred up by the pope's enemy faction, rose up in arms. Robert Guiscard then came to the aid of Gregory VII. Protected by his arms, Gregory was forced to flee and went into voluntary exile in Salerno, where he renewed the excommunication of Henry and antipope Clement. He died there soon after, on 24 May 1085. It is said that his last words may have been: *"Dilexi iustitiam, propterea morior in exilio"* ("I have loved justice, therefore I die in exile") recalling the words of the psalmist: "Thou hast loved justice, and hated iniquity: therefore God, thy God, hath anointed thee with the oil of gladness above thy fellows" (Psalm 44:8).

While Gregory VII was forced into exile, on 2 July 1084 the forces of Countess Matilda of Tuscany unexpectedly defeated the imperial army in the battle of Sorbara near Modena, and succeeded in forming a coalition favourable to the papacy and opposing the Imperial League. She died in July 1115 after a forty-year reign, thirty years after Gregory, whose faithful defender she had always been. In the seventeenth century her body was transferred to Saint Peter's Basilica, where it still rests today.

It was also thanks to a strong woman like Matilda of Tuscany that Gregory VII, apparently defeated, triumphed with the strength of his evangelical message. This demonstrated the importance of the spiritual bonds that have often connected the saints to each other in the course of history.

The message of Saint Gregory VII is summarised in these words of his correspondence:

"God is our witness that against depraved sovereigns and ungodly priests no personal convenience nor any worldly respect spurred us on, but rather the consideration of our office and power of the Apostolic See, about which we are distressed every day. It is better for us to face, if necessary, the due death of the flesh at the hands of tyrants rather than consenting by our silence, out of fear or convenience, to the ruin of the Christian law. We know in fact that our holy Fathers said: 'Whoever, in consideration of his office, does not oppose evil men, it is as if he consented to them: and whoever does not eliminate evils which ought to be repressed, it is as if he committed them.'"

5. What is the reform of the Church?

The so-called investiture struggle, that is, the battle between the Roman Church and the empire for the investiture of bishops and the conferral of ecclesiastical benefices, lasted from the pontificate of Gregory VII until the Concordat of Worms in 1122.

The term "investiture", which appeared only in the eleventh century, refers to the consignment of the symbols of the ring and crosier to the elected bishop. Thus the problem of investiture does not involve the designation of the bishop but the granting of power.

According to Catholic doctrine, the bishop is the successor of the apostles in the ordinary government of particular Churches, or dioceses, under the authority of the Roman pontiff. It is historically established that by the beginning of the second century the "monarchical" episcopate was established everywhere as a constitutional norm of the Church founded by the will of God (*iure divino*). Saint Ignatius of Antioch (†107) attests that all of the churches to whom he wrote his letters had only one bishop as a recognised and venerated head.

The first Christian age had established the tradition that the bishops were designated by the clergy, with the agreement of the community of the faithful, and consecrated by the metropolitan of the province or by other bishops. In the age of barbarian domination, the royal power intervened actively in episcopal election. After Charlemagne the *episcopatus* assumed a feudal character. Just as the king invested the count with the civil office (*honor*) along with the related dominions, so the king was given the power to invest the bishop both in the rights attached to the episcopate as well as in religious functions. The fact that the king granted the crosier and also the ring from the middle of the eleventh century, while pronouncing the words *Accipe ecclesiam* signified that the sovereign claimed the attribution of the *episcopatus* in its totality, without distinguishing between the spiritual and the temporal. Theoretically the principle of the canonical election of the bishop remained intact, but it was emptied of its content. The royal concession of the material possession of the bishopric as a fief, of its income, lands, and honours, in practice was transformed into a real conferral of the episcopate as an ecclesiastical office.

Against this interference of secular power, Saint Gregory VII had affirmed the rights of the Church with clarity and vigour. When Guido of Bourgogne, Archbishop of Vienne, was elected pope in 1119 at Cluny, taking the name Callistus II (1119–1124), he referred to the teaching of Gregory VII. From the very beginning of his pontificate he renewed the formal condemnation of investitures as well as the excommunication of Emperor Henry V in a great synod held in Reims in the presence of 400 bishops on 29–30 October 1119. As the pope pronounced the words of excommunication, the 400 bishops broke the candles they were holding in their hands in order to emphasise the solemnity of the anathema.

The new pope then dedicated himself to working for the peace of the Church, and after long negotiations he settled on the Concordat of Worms on 23 September 1122, in which it was established that bishops would be elected by the clergy and the people, without imperial intervention, and that, at the moment of taking possession of their lands, bishops would receive temporal investiture from the monarch.

The emperor renounced the investiture of prelates with the ring and crosier (symbols of spiritual authority) while maintaining the right to temporal investiture with the sceptre. The agreement recognised the direct supremacy of the Church on the spiritual plane and her indirect power on the temporal plane. Callistus II was therefore able to hold the Ninth Ecumenical Council in the Lateran from 18–27 March 1123, which was also the first assembly of all the bishops held in the West (the preceding Ecumenical Councils had all taken place in the East). At this Council, the agreement between Church and empire was solemnly confirmed, ecclesiastical discipline was restored with a series of canons against simony and in favour of the celibacy of priests, and the holy war against the Saracens was promoted.

At this point one may ask: What was the essential nature of the reform of the Church from which all this sprang? It must be answered that the reform was the rectification of behaviour and the elimination of the abuses which had spread with the passing of time; it was the return to the primitive spirit which had been lost and to the original laws that had been forgotten; it was the rediscovery of a lost identity. Whoever carries out the work of reform is searching for his true self. He wants to replace the old man with the new man, but he is still the same man, not another man.

Reform, when it is authentic, is inspired by the Holy Ghost and the collaboration between divine grace and the human will which corresponds to grace. Reform is opposed to revolution: reform is continuity with the past, while revolution is a cutting and fracturing between the past and present. Protestantism presented itself as a reform of the Church, but it was a revolution initiated within the Church that ended outside of her and against her. Reform is progress that does not deny the tradition of the Church but rather is nourished by it; reform is by definition a return to the tradition in doctrine, in spirit, and in customs. All that which, in the name of a pseudo-reform, is opposed to tradition is in reality revolution and, as such, must be fought against.

Saint Gregory VII in the eleventh century, Saint Pius V in the sixteenth century, and Saint Pius X in the twentieth century were all great reforming popes and great defenders of the tradition. It is moving to read the letters of two saints: Blessed Cardinal Alfredo Ildefonso Schuster and Saint Giovanni Calabria, who hoped for a profound reform of the Church in the 1950s, the years preceding the Second Vatican Council, also proposing a "reform" of the Church which did not reach its goal.

The pontificate of Saint Gregory VII offers us the model of an authentic spiritual and moral reform of the Church, based also on the fullness of power of the Successor of Peter. From this spirit of Gregorian and Cluniac reform, to the cry of *Deus vult!* (God wills it), was born the epic history of the Crusades.

Historians connect the First Crusade, called by the Cluniac Pope Urban II, to the great movement of reform of the Church of the eleventh century. From then on — until Saint Catherine of Siena's calls for reform and at the same time for a Crusade — the idea of the Crusade would be inseparable from that of the renewal of the society and of the Church. The militant spirit of the Crusades and the spirit of penance of the reformers was born from the love of the same Cross that the hedonism of the time rejected, just as our own time rejects it one thousand years later. And once again, only in love for the Cross will the means for a profound reform of the Church be found, a reform which is also a Crusade against her internal and external enemies.

Radio Maria, 21 March 2012

CHAPTER IX
The spirit of the Crusades

1. The origin of the Crusades

The Crusades represent the culmination of the new civilisation which arose at the dawn of the year 1000.

By "Crusades" we mean, in the strict sense, the military expeditions undertaken by the papacy for the liberation of the Holy Sepulchre between the eleventh and thirteenth centuries. At a historical level they may be considered to have begun with the Council of Piacenza in 1095, at which Blessed Urban II issued his first appeal for the Crusade, and to have concluded with the fall of Saint John of Acre, the last Christian outpost in the Holy Land, in 1291.

In a wider sense, the Crusades may be understood simply as armed endeavours undertaken in defence of the faith and of Christian civilisation. In this sense, the Crusades also include the

Spanish *Reconquista* against the Moors, which developed for eight hundred years between the Battle of Covadonga in 722 and the fall of Granada in 1492, as well as the battles of Lepanto (1571), Vienna (1683), and Budapest (1686) in the following centuries. The Crusades in the strict sense, however, were something other and something greater. At Covadonga and Lepanto the Christian knights fought to defend their faith, but also their own countries, which were threatened by Islam. However, the war in the Holy Land was conducted for pre-eminently spiritual reasons. It was not a war of aggression undertaken to impose faith, like those of Islam. There were never forced conversions imposed by the Crusaders.

What the Crusaders sought was only the liberation of the holy places which by law belonged to the Christians and had been unduly occupied by the Muslims. It is important to emphasise this: the principal goal of the Crusades was never political or economic, but it was always pre-eminently religious: the reconquest of the Holy Land or, later, the preservation of the Christian kingdom of Jerusalem which was created by the First Crusade. If the Spanish *Reconquista* and the Holy League supported by Saint Pius V and Blessed Innocent XI were truly noble undertakings, then the epic of the Crusades must be considered to be still more so, and it emerges even now as one of the most illustrious pages in the history of the Church.

In order to understand the origin of the Crusades, we must above all recall the very close bond that existed in the first millennium between Europe and the Holy Land. During the reign of Emperor Constantine, his mother, Empress Helena went to the land where Jesus Christ was born, lived, and died for human salvation. There she discovered the wood of the True Cross and many other important relics. Since then, neither Western nor Eastern Christians have ever ceased to make pilgrimages to the Holy Land in order to worship Christ at His Tomb. From the farthest reaches of Gaul and Germany, as well as from the East both near and far,

IX THE SPIRIT OF THE CRUSADES

thousands of Christians flocked to drink from the very sources of their faith. Pilgrims used the maritime route, departing from the ports of the Mediterranean, as well as the land route, which was longer and less safe, crossing the Byzantine Empire, Anatolia, and Syria. These pilgrimages, which crossed rivers and mountains and encountered many difficulties, never ceased even during the age of the barbarian invasions. Indeed, the political and social upheavals of these centuries only made the Holy City of Jerusalem shine with greater light, for it was there that the customs, rites, and memories of Christianity were preserved.

When the armies of King Khosrow of Persia, invaded Syria, Palestine and Egypt in the sixth century, the Holy City of Jerusalem also fell under their control. The conquerors profaned the churches and carried off as booty the relic of the Cross of the Lord which was venerated in the Church of the Resurrection. But the Eastern Emperor Heraclius (610–641) succeeded in conquering the Persians and liberating Jerusalem. He walked through the streets barefoot and carried the wood of the True Cross back to the summit of Calvary. He considered this relic the most glorious trophy of his victories.

However, far worse misfortunes awaited the Christians. At the beginning of the seventh century the religion of Mohammed had arisen, who promised his disciples that they would conquer the world. After taking over Persia and Syria, the Mohammedans occupied Egypt and from there reached the shores of the Atlantic. In 638 Jerusalem was taken by the Caliph Omar (682–720), the successor of the "prophet". For the Muslims, Jerusalem was a sacred city, because they said that Mohammed was brought there by the Archangel Gabriel during a nocturnal journey and then had been transported to the throne of Allah in paradise.

In the lands subject to Islam, Christians had the status of *dhimmi* and were deprived of their principal rights. They were able to continue practising their religion, but only in private, without being able to spread it or to criticise the Muslim religion. As Christians they always had to be subjected to the Islamic conquerors, to whom they had to pay a special tax. They were even forbidden to ride horses or bear arms. A sign of their condition as *dhimmi* was a leather belt which they were never to take off. But pilgrims continued to flow into the Holy Land, remembering that Jesus had been loaded down with chains and had died on the Cross in the places they went to visit.

At the beginning of the eleventh century, among the Turkmen converted to Islam a new people arose on the Asian steppes under a leader named Seljuk (c.1010). His descendants, who were named the Seljuks after him, occupied Persia and Iraq. In 1071 the Seljuk Sultan of Baghdad defeated the Byzantine army in the Battle of Manzikert, capturing the Eastern Emperor Romanos IV (c.1030–1072). Following this victory, the Muslims occupied the majority of the Asian provinces of Byzantium. The situation of relative tolerance toward the Christians was brutally changed, and the Turks now set out to conquer Byzantium.

The Byzantine Empire now experienced a phase of decline. At Constantinople after the reign of Heraclius, eleven emperors were slain in the palace, six withdrew to monasteries, and many were mutilated, blinded, and exiled. Corruption seemed to destroy an empire that over the centuries had become ever more distant from Rome, until it had provoked a religious schism. Meanwhile, a new Holy Empire had arisen in the West, first under Charlemagne and then under the Ottos of Germany.

At the beginning of the year 1000, Byzantium seemed to be in her old age, while Europe was living her tumultuous youth, as manifested in the movement of spiritual reform that emerged from the abbey of Cluny.

As soon as he was elected pope, Saint Gregory VII, who was formed at Cluny, began to conceive great plans to raise a Christian army against the Turks. In his eyes, the liberation of the holy places represented the culmination of the reform of the Church to which he dedicated his entire pontificate.

During these years, a pilgrim of unknown origin named Peter the Hermit began to travel through France, preaching in fiery words about the need to assist the Christians of the East. He had been in Jerusalem and was moved by the miserable condition into which the holy places had fallen. The old patriarch of Jerusalem had said to him in tears, "Asia is in the hands of the Muslims; the whole East has fallen into slavery. No earthly power can help us." Peter replied to him by swearing that he would do everything he could to convince the warriors of the West to intervene.

Peter the Hermit met Pope Urban II (1088–1099) in Rome, then crossed the Alps and made his way through France. He travelled on a mule, covered by a cloak of rough cloth, holding a crucifix. He preached with an impetuous eloquence from city to city, describing the living conditions of the Christians of the East and calling Western Christians to liberate the Holy Land.

At the same time, the Eastern Emperor Alexios I Komnenos (1081–1118) sent an embassy to Urban II to plead the cause of Constantinople, which was in danger of falling under the terrible domination of the Turks.

Pope Urban II, who like Gregory VII had been spiritually formed by the ideals of Cluny, was keenly sensitive to this subject. In March 1095, he held a Council at Piacenza at which he announced his decision to convene a synod in order to issue an appeal to Christendom.

2. Urban II and the Council of Clermont

The Council was held in the French city of Clermont in November 1095. The city was barely able to contain all the princes, ambassadors, and prelates who flocked there from every part of Christian

Europe. The assembly, under the direction of the pope, began by dealing with the reform of the clergy and ecclesiastical discipline, and then moved on to addressing the internal life of Christendom. One of its decrees placed widows, orphans, workers, and all the weakest members of the population under the protection of the Church. Then in the tenth session, on 27 November, Urban II addressed the expected subject of a holy war.

Peter the Hermit, who was seated at the pope's side, spoke first, describing the profanations and sacrileges he had witnessed. Then Pope Urban II spoke. He too spoke about the outrages against the Christian faith and concluded with a vibrant peroration:

> "People of the Franks, people from over the mountains, people chosen and loved by God, as shines out in many of your actions, distinguished from all nations both by the site of your country as well as by your observance of the Catholic faith and the honour you show to the Holy Church, our speech and our exhortation are addressed to you.
>
> "We want you to know what a gloomy reason has brought us to your lands, what need of you and all the faithful has drawn us here. From Jerusalem and from Constantinople, painful news has reached us, more than once: the Muslims, a people so different from us, a people completely alien to God, a race with an inconstant heart whose spirit has not been faithful to the Lord, have invaded the lands of those Christians, ravaged them with iron, robbery, and fire, and they have led a portion of the inhabitants of these lands away as prisoners to their own country. Another portion they have killed with wretched slaughter, and the churches of God they have either destroyed from the foundations or have used them for the worship of their own religion."

IX THE SPIRIT OF THE CRUSADES

After describing the massacres perpetrated by the Muslims, the pope continued:

> "Who therefore bears the burden of taking revenge and reconquering these lands, if not you to whom more than all other peoples God has granted eminent glory in arms, greatness of soul, agility in your limbs, and the power to humiliate to the very end those who resist you?
>
> "May the deeds of your ancestors move and incite you, the honesty and grandeur of your King Charlemagne, Louis his son, and your other sovereigns who destroyed the pagan kingdoms and extended the boundaries of the Church to include them. Above all, may you be spurred on by the Holy Sepulchre of Our Saviour, and all the holy places, which are now shamefully possessed by an unclean people and irreverently soiled by its filth. O most brave soldiers, sons of invincible fathers, do not be degenerate but recall the valour of your predecessors, and if you are held back by the sweet affection of children, parents and spouses, go back to what the Lord says in the Gospel: 'Whoever loves father and mother more than me, is not worthy of me. Whoever leaves father or mother or wife or children or lands for the love of my name will receive a hundred times more and will possess eternal life.' ... Let the divisions among you cease, let all quarrels be silenced, let wars be placated and all dissension and enmity be appeased. Take the way of the Holy Sepulchre, snatch that land from that wicked people and subject it to you: it was given by God to the children of Israel as a possession; as the scripture says, milk and honey flow in it.
>
> "O most beloved brothers, today what the Lord says in the Gospel has been manifested: 'Where two or three are gath-

ered in my name, I am in the midst of them.' If the Lord God had not inspired your thoughts, your voice would not have been unanimous; although it resounded with different ways of speech, it nevertheless had only one origin: God raised it up, God inspired your hearts. So let this voice of yours be your battle cry, since it comes from God.

"When you go to assault the warlike enemies, may this be the unanimous cry of all the soldiers of God: 'God wills it! God wills it!'"

The assembly of the faithful, carried away with supernatural enthusiasm, responded to the pope's words with a unanimous cry: 'God wills it! God wills it!'"

Cardinal Gregorio (who would later become Pope Innocent II) spoke a formula of general confession in a loud voice. Then all present knelt down, struck their breast, and received absolution for their sins. Following this, all placed a red cross of cloth or silk on their clothing. Adhemar di Monteuil, the bishop of Puy-en-Velay, who had been a knight before his ordination as a priest, was the first to take the Cross from the hands of the pope. Bishops, barons, and knights imitated his example. From that time on, those who pledged to fight the infidels were called "Crusaders".

The Christians who responded to the appeal of Urban II considered themselves pilgrims in arms. The pope introduced the vow of the Crusade, which could only be fulfilled by arrival in the Holy Land, and he granted to the participants, as to those who fought the Moors in Spain, the remission of the earthly penalties imposed by the Church on sinners, with the difference that in Spain the indulgence was granted only to those who died in battle, while in the East it was granted also to those who survived. This is the origin of the plenary indulgence.

IX THE SPIRIT OF THE CRUSADES

Urban II also placed the persons, families, and possessions of the Crusaders under the protection of the Church and Saints Peter and Paul. According to the decrees of the Council of Clermont, the Crusaders were exempt from taxes, nor could they be sued for debts during their expedition. The historian of the Crusades Joseph-François Michaud, from whose account we are drawing, writes: "It seemed that the French had no other homeland than the Holy Land ... The fire which lit up France spread: to England, still agitated by the recent conquest of the Normans; to Germany, troubled by the excommunications of Gregory and Urban; to Italy, torn apart by factions; and to Spain itself, which was fighting the Saracens on its own territory."

The appeal of Urban II had given birth to a great religious movement destined to survive for centuries. The Crusader army was a tumultuous and colourful crowd, offering a spectacle of warriors of all backgrounds and conditions. Michaud writes:

> "Near the cities, outside the fortresses, in the plains, on the mountains, tents and pavilions sprang up for the knights, and altars were arranged in the best way to celebrate the Divine Office; everywhere preparations for war and feast days were in full swing. On the one hand there was the clang of arms and the blaring of trumpets, on the other psalms and canticles. From the Tiber to the Atlantic and from the Rhine to beyond the Pyrenees, one saw only troops of armies decorated with the cross who were singing their conquests in advance, vowing to exterminate the Saracens. In every place the war-cry of the Crusaders rang out: 'God wills it! God wills it!'"

At the Council of Clermont Urban II fixed the feast of the Assumption of the following year, 15 August 1096, as the departure date for the Crusaders. The plan was for the princes and captains who led the armies to take different routes and meet in Constantinople. But in the spring of 1096 a disorganised mass of the faithful under the leadership of Peter the Hermit and Gautier Sans-Avoir departed from the banks of the Meuse and the Moselle and headed for the Bosphorus without waiting for the departure of the princes with their feudal armies.

On their journey they crossed the lands of the Hungarians and the Bulgarians, who had recently embraced Christianity but lived on the fringes of Christendom and had preserved their ferocious customs. They had violent clashes with them, partly due to their own imprudence. The members of the disorganised mass were either dispersed or exterminated between the Danube and the plains of Bithynia. Peter the Hermit escaped death, but Gautier Sans-Avoir was slain in an ambush along with the army he had rallied. The "People's Crusade", as it was called, ended in failure.

Meanwhile, towards the middle of August 1096, the second wave of Crusaders began to leave Western Europe. This time it was a disciplined army led by the best knights in Christendom. From Central Europe came Robert, Count of Flanders, who was at the head of the Frisians and Flemings, and Godfrey of Bouillon, the Duke of Lower Lorraine, with his brothers Baldwin and Eustace, and their cousin Baldwin of Bourg. The French had their champion in Count Hugh of Vermandois, the brother of King Philip. The Norman princes were led by Robert, the eldest son of William the Conqueror, and by the Hautevilles, descendants of Robert Guiscard, who had conquered Puglia and Calabria and protected Saint Gregory VII against Emperor Henry IV. Among the Normans, Bohemond, the prince of Taranto, stands out, whom the authors of the time describe as being exceptionally tall and equally extraordinary in his mastery of arms. Bohemond would prove to be the best strategist in the army but also the most ambitious. With him was his nephew Tancred of Hauteville, the most dedicated

IX THE SPIRIT OF THE CRUSADES

to religion and honour after Godfrey. Tancred's biographer says that for a long time he wavered between the maxims of the world and those of the Gospel, but once the holy war was proclaimed, nothing could stop his warlike momentum. Another man who took up the Crusader's cross was Stephen, Count of Blois and Chartres, who was considered among the richest lords of his time, so much so that it was said of him that he had as many castles as there are days in the year. The faithful asked for the pope to place himself at their head, but he chose as his apostolic legate Bishop Adhemar of Le Puy, while Raymond of Saint-Giles, Count of Toulouse, was appointed as military head. He was a 55-year-old warrior who had had the honour of fighting in Spain alongside El Cid. He had defeated the Moors many times under Alfonso the Great, who had given him his daughter Elvira in marriage.

But the most prominent figure of the Crusades, both for his astonishing physical strength as well as for his purity of manners and prudence in command, was Godfrey of Bouillon. Once in Syria some Arab sheiks, in order to put him to the test, challenged him to behead an adult camel — an animal until then unknown in the west — with a single sword stroke: immediately the head of the animal rolled at their feet. Michaud writes that "he was always ready to dedicate himself to the cause of the unfortunate and the innocent, and for this reason he was regarded by princes and knights as a model, by soldiers as a father, and by the people as a support".

These were the knights whose exploits have been recounted by many contemporary chroniclers. Many of them were husbands and fathers, proprietors of lands and castles, but they turned their backs generously on everything they had — both earthly affections as well as material goods — convinced only that they were going to meet an uncertain destiny, entrusted only to the designs of divine providence. This alone is enough to dispel the legend which says that the Crusades were economic ventures promoted by greedy conquerors, and shows how profoundly spiritual they were.

3. Towards Jerusalem

The Christian army, crossing the Rhône at Lyons, traversed the Alps, Lombardy, and Friuli, and headed towards Greek territory, crossing the wild regions of Dalmatia. Finally, it arrived in Constantinople. The Byzantine emperor had turned to the Latins to help the capital of the empire, but he did not agree with the idea of the Crusade to liberate the Holy Land and feared the presence of such a formidable army in his capital. The dissension between the clergy of Rome and the clergy of Constantinople contributed to the increasing antipathy caused by differences between Eastern and Western habits and customs. The discord provoked frequent clashes and disturbances in which, as Michaud writes, "the Greeks demonstrated more perfidy than valour and the Latins more valour than moderation".

Finally, the Crusaders left Constantinople to head towards the fortified city of Nicea, in Bithynia, famous for the two ancient Councils that had been held there, and which had now become the capital of the Turkish Sultanate. The Muslims, since they were in an advanced position, were awaiting the opportunity to assault Constantinople and then overthrow Europe. The spectacle of the advancing Crusader army was majestic and terrible: there were tens of thousands of knights and foot soldiers who camped in front of the city of Nicea, which was protected by an incalculable number of towers and moats. The chronicler wrote, "I do not believe that anyone has ever seen or ever will see so many valiant knights." Fulcher of Chartres, one of those present, counted nineteen Christian nations in the field, each with their own language and set of customs. Each had its own area, marked off by walls and palisades. Since there were no stones or wood for entrenchments, they used

IX THE SPIRIT OF THE CRUSADES

the bones of the Christians who had been massacred by the Turks during the People's Crusade, which had remained unburied in the fields near Nicea.

The Crusaders used spears, swords, daggers, and iron clubs, but also the bow and crossbow: a weapon until that time unknown to the easterners. The princes and knights carried colourful images and signs on their banners, which served to keep the soldiers together. These insignia are at the origin of the titles and coats of arms of western nobility that were born on the battlefields of the Crusades. There is still no greater title of glory for a noble than to be descended from Crusader blood.

A year had passed since their departure when, before the walls of Nicea on 21 May 1097, the Crusaders had their first victory. The battle lasted the entire day and the victory cost the Christians two thousand men. The Saracens however retreated in disorder to the mountains, leaving four thousand dead in the plain. From that moment the siege of Nicea became ever more stringent. The fortress was beginning to falter, but the intrigues of the Byzantine Emperor Alexios took the glory of victory away from the Crusaders. Alexios negotiated with the Turks for the surrender of the city, and just as the Crusaders were preparing for the final assault, the banner of the Byzantine emperor suddenly appeared on the walls and towers of Nicea. By treating the Turkish prisoners with excessive generosity, Alexios showed the Latins that he did not want to go deep into war against his enemies.

The Crusaders did not hide their irritation, but continued their journey through Asia Minor. In the mountains of Anatolia, the troops were often blocked by narrow passes, streams and precipices. In the plains they were inevitably afflicted by famine, lack of water, and devouring heat. The army was divided into two echelons: the first was led by the princes Bohemond and Tancred, the second by Godfrey of Bouillon and Raymond of Toulouse. On the morning of 1 July 1097, on the plateau of Dorylaeum, the Turks threw themselves *en masse* against Bohemond's army. Despite their valour, the Norman warriors were on the point of succumbing when the other part of the army appeared, led by Raymond of Toulouse and Godfrey of Bouillon. Crushed by the furious charge of the Christian cavalry, the Turks suffered a new defeat, and their camp fell into the hands of the Crusaders, who found immense treasures and above all many camels. After the battle, the Muslim prisoners said that they had seen angels fighting alongside the Crusaders. It was an epic victory that spread the fame of the "Franks", as the Crusaders were now called, from East to West.

The population of Asia Minor was still almost all Christian, and so it favoured the advance of the Franks, saluting them as liberators from the Muslim yoke. One of the principal Crusaders, Baldwin of Flanders, left the army and headed east into Armenia, arriving without a fight in the ancient city of Edessa. There the Greek prince Toros, who governed Edessa as an official vassal of the Turks, named Baldwin as his heir and successor. Shortly afterward an uprising overthrew Toros, and Baldwin found himself lord of the city. He no longer thought of liberating Jerusalem; instead, he wanted to focus solely on his new state. It was a desertion, but, as Michaud observes, the principality of Edessa served to keep the Turks and Saracens in check, and up until the Second Crusade it was the foremost bastion of Christian power in the East.

After crossing the mountain chains of the Taurus and Amanus along narrow and steep paths, on 21 October 1097 the Crusader army arrived before Antioch, where the disciples of Jesus had first been called Christians and whose first bishop had been Saint Peter. According to the ancient authors, Antioch aroused fear because of its immense walls and its four hundred towers and bastions. It was the beginning of winter, and prudence would have dictated that the army wait for the spring to begin its attack, when the weather would be more favourable and reinforcements from both Emperor

Alexios as well as the West would have arrived. But impatience got the upper hand, as often happened during those months, and the Christians attacked the city without having the forces or the siege engines with which to conquer it. Enthusiasm was quickly followed by disappointment once the difficulty of conquering the fortress became evident. Winter was coming, and every day it rained heavily. The Christian camp at the bottom of the valley was submerged by water several times; storms and floods carried away tents and pavilions. Cold and hunger began to claim more and more victims among the soldiers. The knights were forced to kill their horses to feed themselves.

The impregnable city of Antioch fell only thanks to the help of an Armenian renegade named Firuz, who was guarding a tower and opened the city gates from the inside. The conspiracy was organised by Bohemond, who is thus known as "the Ulysses of the Latins". He gathered the other barons and told them that he had the means to take Antioch, on the condition that he would be granted lordship of the city. The coup was carefully prepared by Bohemond himself. On the night of 3 June 1098 his men scaled the walls and opened the gates to their companions, who poured into the city, occupying it in just a few hours.

The city of Antioch fell into the hands of the Crusaders during the first days of June in 1098, after eight months of siege. The following day however a formidable Turkish army, sent by the Seljuks of Persia and commanded by Kerboga, the Emir of Mosul, appeared on the river Orontes. The besiegers who had conquered the city now found themselves under siege, but they were exhausted by hunger and fatigue. The famine in the city was terrible. The situation seemed desperate, so much so that one of the leaders, Stephen of Blois, who was outside the city of Antioch, on seeing the extent of the Turkish encampment from the nearby heights, convinced himself that everything was lost and started heading back to France. The entire West was indignant at his abandonment of the battlefield. Recounting how Stephen of Blois died in battle during the Second Crusade, William of Tyre said that God made his mercy shine on him, because only death could redeem the shame of desertion.

It happened, however, that a Provençal Christian, Pietro Bartolomeo, proclaimed that Saint Andrew had appeared to him and had revealed the location of the Holy Lance, the weapon with which Longinus had pierced the side of Christ. Bartolomeo himself was said to have found a spearhead under the slabs of the floor of the Cathedral of Saint Peter, and this discovery galvanised the Crusaders, who saw in it the foretelling of their imminent victory. The Emir Kerboga was certain of his military superiority. Imagine his astonishment when, on the feast of Saints Peter and Paul, he saw the gates of the city of Antioch, which he thought to be conquered, open up and the entire Crusader army pour out in full arms — divided into twelve corps representing the twelve apostles. In the first rows, Hugh the Great carried the standard of the Church, although he was weakened by a long illness. All the princes, knights and barons led their men, except for Raymond of Toulouse who was wounded. They were preceded by Bishop Adhemar dressed in armour and full pontifical vestments. Exhausted by hunger and fatigue, the Crusaders, as Michaud writes, were sustained only by the hope of either winning or dying.

The countryside around Antioch was covered with Muslim warriors, whose leader Kerboga appeared invincible. It was an epic clash, but the Muslims were overwhelmed by the impetus of the Crusaders. Kerboga, who had already announced the defeat of the Christians to the Caliph of Baghdad and the Sultan of Persia, fled at full speed towards the Euphrates.

The monk Robert recounts that in the midst of the fray a white militia was seen descending from heaven, led by the martyr saints George, Demetrios, and Theodore. According to the accounts of several historians, the infidels lost one hundred thousand men in the field, and the Crusaders lost four thousand, who were numbered among the martyrs.

The weather was very hot, and the Crusaders decided to stop at Antioch until the end of autumn. But in the following months many of them fell victim to a grave epidemic. Adhemar of Puy also succumbed to it, and like Moses he died without seeing the Promised Land.

More than 200,000 men had departed Europe in the Crusader army. Most of these died in battle or through hunger or disease. The army that would set out from Antioch to accomplish the conquest of the holy places numbered less than 50,000 combatants. But this did not stop them from pursuing their goal.

4. The liberation of the Holy City

In January 1099, the Crusaders resumed their march towards Jerusalem. The way was long and punctuated with skirmishes and battles of secondary importance, until spring came. The crops covered the fields, and the Christian soldiers saw the mountains of Lebanon rising in the distance as they made their way. Between the mountains and the sea, the countryside they crossed was covered with tall olive trees. Skirting the sea, the Crusaders came to the walls of ancient Ptolemais, which they would rechristen as Saint John of Acre. Next, they occupied Lydda, the ancient Diospolis, famous for the martyrdom of Saint George. Before the cities of Beirut, Tyre, and Saint John of Acre the terrified local emirs offered them the supplies they needed, while other Muslims hurried to Jerusalem to defend it with all their might. When they reached the hill of Emmaus, Godfrey of Bouillon sent his cousin Baldwin of Bourg and Tancred de Hauteville with one hundred knights towards Bethlehem, where the Saviour was born. The Christians of the city, who were the great majority, came out in procession with their crosses and books of the Gospel to welcome the liberators after four centuries of oppression. Led by the jubilant people, Tancred and his companions went to the Church of the Nativity and, as the chronicler recounts, "they saw the manger where the sweet Child, who created heaven and earth, had rested". Finally, on 6 June 1099, the standard of Tancred was planted on top of the Basilica of the Virgin.

On that same night, a sudden eclipse covered the earth in darkness, while a blood-red veil hid the moon. No one slept, and at dawn the Crusaders, having now come just a few miles from Jerusalem, resumed their journey with enthusiasm. When the sun appeared on the horizon the entire army advanced with unfurled banners, and the domes of the Holy City revealed themselves before their eyes. From the front rows came cries of "Jerusalem! Jerusalem!" The name flew from mouth to mouth. The cries were repeated by 40,000 armed pilgrims and echoed over Zion and the Mount of Olives. The knights descended from their horses to advance on foot: everyone repeated their oath to liberate the Holy City from the sacrilegious dominion of the Muslims. Once they arrived under the city walls, the Crusaders divided up into sectors of attack. Robert of Normandy took the northern sector, facing the Gate of Damascus; Robert of Flanders was in front of the eastern gate, which is now Notre Dame of France; Godfrey of Bouillon and Tancred were in the western sector where the Jaffa Gate and the Citadel are; and finally Raymond of Toulouse took the south, on Mount Zion.

It was the middle of June and the heat was stifling: there was no water, and above all there were no ladders or siege engines, both of which were necessary to take the city. On 13 June, a first attack was attempted, but the Crusaders were easily repulsed. However, almost miraculously a small Genoan fleet arrived in Jaffa, carrying food supplies and building materials. The Crusaders immediately set to work building catapults, large ladders, and wooden towers

IX THE SPIRIT OF THE CRUSADES

on wheels with which to approach the city walls. It was long and gruelling work because of the heat.

On 8 July, the Muslims, watching from the height of the city walls, were surprised to see the Crusader army, barefoot and unarmed, walking around the Holy City intoning prayers. Finally, on 14 July 1099 the trumpets blared in the Christian camp: all the Crusaders ran to arms, and all the siege engines moved forward at the same moment. From atop the battlements the Muslims let fly a shower of arrows, fire, and boiling oil over the Crusaders as they tried to climb the walls. The violent clash lasted for twelve hours, until night came between the combatants. Suddenly, the Crusaders saw Saint George appear on the Mount of Olives, waving his sword and giving the signal to enter the city. At this point, nothing could stop the onslaught of the Christian fighters.

It was midday on 15 July when Godfrey's tower, advancing in the midst of the tempest of arrows and fire, succeeded in making a walkway over the wall. Godfrey of Bouillon was the first to break into the Holy City, followed by his soldiers, who swept through the city extinguishing every form of resistance in blood. Raymond of Aguilers, an eyewitness, declares that under the portico and atrium of the mosque the blood was knee-deep. Meanwhile, the rumour spread among the Crusaders that Bishop Adhemar and many of his companions who had died during the siege had appeared in the front rows of the attackers and had planted the banner of the Cross on the towers of Jerusalem. The Muslims now fled in every direction, while Jerusalem resounded with the Crusader cry: "God wills it!" It was three in the afternoon on Friday 15 July 1099, the very day and hour in which, in that city, Jesus Christ had died to redeem humanity.

That same evening, the Crusaders, as the chronicler recounts, "washed their hands and feet, changed their bloody garments for new clothes, and went barefoot to the holy places". Gathered on Calvary in the silence of the night, the Christian army demonstrated such piety that it seemed, as has been written, that these men, rather than having just come out of a terrifying massacre, had spent their lives in meditation in a hermitage.

The last battle of the First Crusade was fought in Ascalon on 12 August 1099 against a greatly superior enemy. "The battle was fierce," the chronicler continues, "but the divine strength accompanied us in such a great and powerful way that we soon annihilated them. The enemies of God were blind and astonished: although their eyes were open, it was as if they could not see the knights of Christ and did not dare to oppose them, because they were terrified of the divine power."

Now the holy city needed to be governed. Godfrey of Bouillon was chosen from the Crusaders. The ancient chronicles compare him to a lion on the battlefield and a monk in everyday life. He refused to accept the title of king of the place where Our Lord had carried the crown of thorns, and desired instead to be called defender and first "advocate of the Holy Sepulchre". It was only after his death that his brother Baldwin I (1100–1118), who succeeded him, took the title of Christian King of Jerusalem on Christmas Day of the year 1100.

The Crusader army had marched thousands of miles amidst all kinds of difficulties, had defeated the main Turkish and Egyptian armies, and had reconquered the Holy City of Jerusalem for the first time in 450 years. It was a historic defeat for Islam. For the West, it set an example that would endure down the centuries.

5. The Crusades as a category of the spirit

There were seven Crusades, or eight, depending on how one counts them. They witnessed acts of extraordinary natural and supernatural heroism, undertaken by heroes like Baldwin IV (1161–1185), known as the Leper King, who was disfigured by illness and fought on a litter, and Saint Louis IX (1214–1270), the model of the perfect Christian knight.

The most perfect expression of the Crusades were the military religious orders like the Knights of Saint John, later called the Knights of Malta, the Teutonic Knights, and above all the Templars, whose rule was written by Saint Bernard of Clairvaux (1090–1153) and approved by the Church. Catholics who criticise the Crusades, must first of all keep in mind that the Crusades were always advocated, organised and directed by the Church, which considered the Crusader army as its own army. The popes were recognised as the heads of each Crusade, but since they could not personally participate, they had themselves represented by a papal legate who, although he did not direct the military operations, played an important role of counsel and was the supreme authority of the army, under the guidance of the pope.

There is a close connection between the Crusades and martyrdom. But the epic of the Crusades is, in a certain respect, superior even to the epic of the martyrs, because martyrdom is a supreme test which comes suddenly. One must make a dramatic choice: either fidelity to Christ, who opens the gates of paradise, or the cowardice of apostasy, which opens the gates of hell. And those who do not have a heroic vocation also have the duty of bearing witness, even to the shedding of blood.

The Crusade, unlike martyrdom, is a choice that implies the heroic vocation of a life dedicated to the battle for the Church and Christian civilisation. This means being ready to die not only on actual battlefields, but in all the harsh trials of daily life. In the various expeditions to liberate the Holy Sepulchre, the number of those who fell by fatigue, hunger, and disease was greater than those who died in combat, to say nothing of the terrible spiritual and moral trials that were endured: distance from loved ones, uncertainty about the future, and being misunderstood by brother Christians, and at times even betrayed by them.

The philosophy of the Crusades is antithetical to a certain ecumenical spirit that has spread among Christians. Today it is believed that good and evil have the same rights, and religious liberty is understood as the right of all religions to claim that they are true. The Crusades, on the other hand, presuppose a Christian theology that says that evil and error have no right to reign, and there is no other truth outside Jesus Christ and His Gospel, the only Way, Truth, and Life (Jn 14:6).

Those who are convinced of this must desire with all their might that evil be extirpated from society and that good alone may triumph: they must desire this with a greater intensity than those who believe, in the name of relativism, that the Christian roots of society must be eradicated, using force if necessary.

For this reason, Saint Bernard writes with theological certainty in the Rule he gave to the Knights Templar, *De Laude Novae Militiae*:

> "The knights of Christ can with tranquillity of conscience fight the battles of the Lord, without either fear of death or of sin in killing the enemy, since in either kind of death — inflicted or suffered for Christ — there is nothing criminal and it often brings the merit of glory. In fact, as with the former one gives glory to Christ, so with the latter one obtains Christ Himself. Without a doubt He gladly accepts the death of the enemy as punishment, and even more gladly does he give Himself to the soldier as consolation. The knight of Christ kills with a tranquil conscience and dies with even greater security. By dying he favours himself; by killing he favours Christ. It is not without reason that the soldier carries the sword. He is the minister of God for the punishment of the wicked and the exaltation of the good. When he kills a wicked man, he is not a murderer, but rather a 'malicide' [one who kills evil]. It is necessary to see in him both the avenger who is at the service of Christ as well as

the defender of the Christian people. Then when he dies, we must not think that he is dead, but rather that he has reached eternal glory."

Of course, it is necessary to distinguish the error from the one who errs. But if Our Lord has shed His Blood for every creature, He has also shed it so that His Kingdom may triumph over society. And in order for this to happen, alongside the God of mercy, which the many religious orders dedicated to charity and service have represented, there is also the God of justice, represented by the Crusaders and all those in history who have dedicated their life to fighting evil and errors, responding to those words of the Gospel which comfort us greatly but must also spur us on to the fight: "Seek ye first the kingdom of God and his justice, and all these things shall be added unto you" (Mt 6:33).

Radio Maria, 18 April 2012

THE CHURCH IN THE TEMPESTS

www.ingramcontent.com/pod-product-compliance
Lightning Source LLC
Chambersburg PA
CBHW030259100526
44590CB00012B/454